Gonville ffrench-Beytagh was born in Shanghai in 1912, the son of an Irish businessman. After the break-up of his parents' marriage, he was sent to England to be brought up by a parson's daughter, Esylt Newbery. Then, as an adolescent in New Zealand, he got expelled from school, played hide-and-seek with the police, and for three years wandered over the country as a tramp and casual labourer. In his twenties he went to work in Johannesburg and there the example of friends attracted him to Christianity and almost immediately into the priesthood.

For twenty-five years he alternately infuriated and inspired the ecclesiastical establishment in South Africa and Rhodesia, eventually becoming Dean of Salisbury in 1954 and then Dean of Johannesburg in 1964. It was while he was in the latter position that his name hit the headlines when the South African police arrested him because of his anti-apartheid activities. The story of his arrest, trial, conviction and final release is told in detail in the autobiographical *Encountering Darkness*.

Since returning to England Canon ffrench-Beytagh has been lecturing and preaching at universities and theological colleges here and in America and Canada. He is the Warden of the Servants of Christ the King and has been made an honorary canon of Canterbury Cathedral. After a year as assistant curate of St Matthew's in Westminster he took up, in April 1974, his present position as rector of a City church, St Vedast-alias-Foster.

By the same author

ENCOUNTERING DARKNESS

ENCOUNTERING LIGHT

Gonville ffrench-Beytagh

FONTANA/Collins

First published in Fontana Books 1975
© G. A. ffrench-Beytagh 1975
Made and printed in Great Britain by
William Collins Sons & Co Ltd, Glasgow

Biblical quotations in this book are taken
from the Authorized Version

*This book has been edited by Alison Norman
from material which I provided*

G.A.ff.-B

Contents

CHAPTER ONE

'Rooted and grounded in love'

What distinguishes a Christian from anybody else is not that he goes to church, or that he is good, or that he has been baptized, but that he knows that he, John Smith, is loved and valued at a depth beyond any human imagining and that he desires to respond to that love. He may feel almost filled with hate and lust and envy but he knows he is loved – the whole of him, not just the 'good' bits – and so he can begin to open himself to God and his fellow-men and allow the power of divine love to flood through him.

There can be no bounds to that love. The Bible says 'God so loved the world . . .' It does not say 'God so loved the Church' (God must get terribly fed up with the Church at times, as most of us do). And it does not say that God so loved the poor or the rich, or the Whites or the Blacks, or any particular nation or class or creed, or even human beings by themselves. God so loved the whole creation and every being in it that he gave himself for it. Each of us, every single individual, is treasured in God's love, and it is obvious, when one comes to think about it, that if any one individual is loved, then the whole universe must be loved also. For there is a unity in creation. Our individual bodies are made of the stuff of the universe, deriving their being ultimately from the unimaginable origins of all matter, and we are dependent for every moment of our physical existence on sun and air and water and on our membership of the body of mankind, with a cultural and genetic inheritance stretching back to the first life on earth. If we want to open ourselves to the love of

God, we must accept our utter involvement with all other men, whatever their colour or creed may be.

But love is not the sentimental easy feeling which the world thinks it is. Love can be painful, bloody and terrifying. As St Paul says, it *suffers*; it strips us as naked mentally as sexual intercourse strips us physically; it is not smooth and sweet and soothing – the love of romantic novelists and cooers over babies in prams; it is coping with a baby who screams for weeks on end and perhaps grows up a helpless, dribbling, mentally handicapped cripple; it is the struggle to keep a marriage alive and growing, not for five years but for fifty, perhaps through mental illness and unfaithfulness and inhuman housing conditions and the sheer boredom of sameness. Love is being able to tell the truth when this is necessary even if it will hurt most bitterly, as Jesus so often did, and being willing to face unpopularity, contempt and the pain of people who cannot understand. In many countries today it can mean torture, imprisonment or death. And so the symbol of love is the cross – one of the most painful and prolonged methods of death by torture which man in his ingenuity has been able to devise: The cross which we make of silver and gold and talk so glibly about 'taking up' and which we hang round our necks. I have often said that I wish Christians today would hang a model of a bedpan round their necks and in their houses. It would convey the menial, smelly, undramatic service which love so often demands more effectively than an ornament whose true meaning we have forgotten.

But love is also *relationship*. It is taking as well as giving. If it is just giving, it is intolerable superiority – a 'Lady Bountiful' *de haut en bas* condescension which Christians have too often mistaken for love and which the world rightly rejects. This kind of giving is generally a way of enabling us to feel 'good' by generating a warm glow of satisfaction and exchanging the costly business of real relationship for the gratitude (even if it is a grudging, resentful gratitude) of those whom we have made dependent on us. If we are truly giving ourselves we will find that we cannot help taking of the other's self and by some mysterious alchemy of love we always receive more than we give. 'Good measure, and shaken together, pressed down, and running over', says Jesus, and it is true. The true lover can never be self-satisfied, because he is always in debt. This is even true, most deeply and mysteriously, of God himself. He does not *need* our love but he does desire it, and he pours himself out for us so that we may have the means to pour ourselves out in him.

All this may sound like hot air – a quite impossible perfectionism which has nothing to do with real human beings – and it is, I believe, true that in some sense Jesus is the only true human being, the only truly normal man – man as he is meant to be. But this generation, more than most, has got itself so bogged down in a slough of despond from looking at all life's difficulties and complications that it often forgets altogether where it is meant to go.

I believe that this despair, and failure, both of which are, God knows, only too real, come because we are trying to fight with the wrong weapons. People think that the kingdom of God can be established by logic and written agreements, by technology, economics, increased production, population control, education, and all the other techniques which we humans have invented. These methods are all important and should be used with as much wisdom and skill as the world can produce, but by themselves, I believe, they are utterly useless.

Behind all the material things which can be manipulated by material techniques, there lies a great brooding evil, a dark satanic power which drags us down and chokes and smothers us in fear, jealousy and pride. 'We wrestle not against flesh and blood, but against principalities, against powers, against the rulers of the darkness of this world, against spiritual wickedness in high places'; against the great basic fears and hates between races, between the exploiter and the exploited, the 'haves' and the 'have-nots'; against the covetousness and selfishness of endless generations: 'What I have I hold', 'What you've got I want'! How can fear and greed be overcome by logic or economics? The forces of darkness have to be fought with the forces of love, and the Christian alone is supernaturally equipped for this war.

'Put on the *whole* armour of God', we are told by St Paul – not little bits here and there, and not just the defensive parts. We need the sword of the Spirit to attack with, as the Cathedral congregation in Johannesburg discovered when I was arrested and held in solitary confinement by the Security Police. They came together and found a new dimension of strength in their spiritual lives through praying for me – it *worked*. I was upheld all through my interrogation by a power which I know was outside myself and I was almost miraculously released after only nine days. But of course, when the crisis was over, the sense of urgent need to pray was lost – and that happens all too often in our individual spiritual lives. We experience the power and strength of the Spirit in some glorious fact of deliverance or healing or some other answered prayer. And then we forget again and life slumps down to its ordinary level of muddling along as best we can under our own steam until some other crisis occurs and we realize once again that by ourselves we are helpless.

I know that talking about the Devil as a person is unfashionable nowadays, and even believing in the powers of evil as a terrible reality is somehow 'not quite nice'. All I can say is that I *know* the Devil is there, from the struggle to get out of bed at the right time in the morning and concentrate properly on my prayers to the struggle not to have 'just one more nightcap' last thing at night, and if you are honest with yourself I believe you will find that you know him too. And you only have to open your newspaper to see his work in the world. He hates real beauty, real joy, real anything, for he is the father of lies who is always whispering to us that the sham is genuine and that what we know to be genuine takes too much effort. 'Bullying, cheating, grabbing, exploiting – that's what life is all about, and if you don't do it you're a fool because everyone else will.' 'Above all, don't *care* – it's all too much bother', and that is one of the most deadly and insidious temptations of all. The Devil will use every weapon he has to make our love grow cold so that we fall back into that easy torpor which is the high road to death.

We can't fight the Devil by ourselves. He is in ourselves and part of ourselves and we have no power against him. Thinking that we can conquer him by ourselves leads to the nastiest kind of moral self-righteousness which is almost as far from true Christianity as it is possible to get (and a lot further away than blatant self-indulgence). The weapons belong to God and not to ourselves, and it is God who will fight for us and within us, if only we can let him.

And so we come back again and again to what I believe is the heart of the Christian life – learning quite literally to be in love, stretching out to 'mystery' at the heart of being, reaching out to each other, growing in obedience and trust and in willingness to bear hurt and drudgery, but above all growing in the certain knowledge that we *are* beloved.

This book is an attempt to explain what being in love means. It is written from my personal experience as a member of the Anglican part of the Church, but there are many other ways of encountering God and I do not believe it matters greatly which one we take.

When I was arrested by the South African Security Police, I had an experience which made me write in my prison diary the words with which I would like to end this chapter:

All this talk too of the 'Goodness of God' – our love being so far below the true Being and Nature of God – they are words which we have to use: just as we have to use

'He' and 'Him': but the unalterable glory is wholly beyond words, concept, vision – everything. And all this is completely impossible to put into words or even into concepts. It is something which is 'given' to man – I have no illusions at all that I receive the Beatific vision or anything like that: I have no vision or visions: but I have a completely satisfying (or almost completely satisfying) knowledge that God *is* (*Encountering Darkness*, p. 263).

CHAPTER TWO

Suicide or adoration

I do not think that there is any chance of beginning to grasp the meaning of love and life without coming to terms with paradox. A paradox is two statements about something which sound contradictory but are in fact both true. And if that sounds double-Dutch, just think about yourself for a minute because you and I and every human being are paradoxical.

We are, on the one hand, animals. We are born, mature and copulate; we eat, excrete and sleep; and finally we die and our bodies rot. But we know for certain inside ourselves that we have something more than this within us. There is something which gets bored to screaming point if only the animal needs are satisfied. Something which cries out for love and the need to belong, and which reaches for the stars or wants to hit out in sheer frustration with the world as it is. Because we are not *just* animals. We are human beings, and human beings are animals *plus* – animals who can love, and see beauty, and create, and long for a reality beyond our senses. We carry in ourselves two apparently contradictory natures, which are both aspects of one reality – and that is exactly what a paradox is. No human being, however saintly, is an angel (that is, a wholly spiritual being) and no human will ever become an angel. We are human beings to all eternity (which is what the doctrine of the resurrection of the body is all about). We are stuck with our mixed-up humanity, and trying to escape from it doesn't work. We can never be wholly spiritual or wholly animal and we can never be some pure amalgamation of the two.

We are *both*. And that is true of all paradoxes. The one thing which you cannot do with a paradox of life is to resolve it. You have got to accept it and live with it and grow through the tension between its two opposite poles – just as we have to with our own human nature.

But of course people do attempt to solve all sorts of paradoxes and there are different ways of trying to cope with the human variety. Some people plug away at trying to find an intelligent answer. They have been taught that if you make the right hypotheses and do the right research it *must* be possible to come up with an answer which will explain what makes a human being human. Unfortunately (or perhaps fortunately) it just doesn't work. The philosophers have given up trying to find meaning in life and the psychologists only find that the more they know about human nature the less they understand it.

Others try to escape from all the frustration of their deepest longings and the boredom of their daily living into their holidays and their days off in their cottage in the country. Heaven is Majorca – holidays are when you become really 'you'. People live for their holidays and they talk about their holidays as 'living it up'. 'I'm alive! This is the real me! For fifty weeks in the year I'm a zombie but here I am free.' (Just pay attention to the words which the tour operators use to advertise their wares and you will see that this is the longing that they are aiming at.) Unfortunately, it doesn't work either, and the more you can afford to 'get away', the less it works. Millionaires are often notoriously unhappy people. You cannot leave your human nature behind by flying to the most exotic beach strewn with even the most luscious blondes.

Another way out is just to become a plum pudding. Some people do their utmost to stifle all that is best in themselves and kid themselves that all they really want is food and warmth and security and someone to go to bed with. What is the use of crying for the moon? Much better to stay safely and firmly on earth and close their minds to those nagging feelings of frustration and dissatisfaction. If they cannot close them completely, there are always dreams – instant beauty offered by a new make-up, the football pools, the weekly horoscope – or, for the more desperate, the pain and frustration can be deadened by alcohol or tranquillizers or other kinds of drugs.

Some braver people make an attempt to face the non-animal parts of themselves, but they do it by trying to deny the animal, earthly side. They try to retreat into the spiritual. Many people today, particularly young people, are turning to various forms of Eastern mysticism, and it seems to me that some of these are based on a denial of the reality of our own natures and life as it is. I believe that we have a great deal to learn from Eastern mysticism – but the proof of the pudding lies in the eating, and I have no doubt that the terrifying neglect of suffering which occurs in so many Eastern countries is in part due to the preoccupation of their spiritual leaders with the supernatural world to the exclusion of the natural one. I say elsewhere in this book that I do not believe that there is any hard-and-fast line between the natural and the supernatural, the physical and the spiritual, but Eastern mysticism does tend to emphasize the spiritual as against the physical needs of man.

This kind of escape is also a common practice among people who adopt various forms of nature mysticism and what might be called the 'escape into beauty'. I think it is true that the great poets, artists and musicians can get closer than most of us to revealing (not resolving) the paradox of life. But it means that they are standing un-aided on the knife-edge of reality, and the cost to their mental and emotional stability can be very great indeed.

None of these methods really work, because our longings are born of our need for God. They have been called 'divine dissatisfaction' – a restlessness which comes from the fact that we were made by God for himself and 'our hearts are restless till they rest in thee'. There can be no meaning or aim in life unless we have a direction in which to steer that is outside ourselves, any more than a sailor can steer without the sun or a star or the magnetic north pole, or some other point of reference which is outside his ship. It is the Christian view that there *is* no direction or purpose in life until God's love becomes both the way and the end. Certainly this was my own experience, as my autobiography, *Encountering Darkness*, makes clear. I did not know who or what I was until I discovered that God loved me – *me* – for myself. Then I found that I mattered, that I had a purpose and a destiny and I was not just a thing, a number on a time-sheet slogging through a monotonous job and the struggle to make ends meet until I ended up as a 'death' in an old people's home.

There is a tendency amongst many people, particularly those with some scientific background, to believe that because the universe is so vast God cannot possibly have any knowledge of all the individuals who live in it. But even we human beings can now build machines which can keep a personal record of millions of people. This was brought home to me when I was travelling in the United States and was shown a vast building near Washington which I was told was known as 'The Martinsville Monster' and which houses a computer system that keeps records of every individual in the United States.

If the Americans can make a machine which can have a personal knowledge, as it were, of every citizen of the United States, it seems to me that it cannot be very difficult for God to have a perfect knowledge of every individual in the world and of whatever other beings in the universe there may be. Machines are only in their infancy and God must be much greater than any machine. So it is my belief, and my experience – as it is the teaching of Christ – that every individual in the world matters. Jesus said such things as 'The very hairs of your head are all numbered', 'A sparrow shall not fall to the ground without your Father knowing', and so on. And I think that unless a person gets hold of the fact that he is unique, he probably will never understand what the Christian religion is about.

Think of yourself for a moment. *There is no one on this earth who is like you.* This may be just as well, but it is true. You may have an identical twin who was removed at birth for all you know, but there is not, and cannot ever have been, nor will there ever be, a person who is exactly like you. Even if someone has exactly the same genes and chromosomes, the environment in which he (or she) grew up will have been different and so he will have become a different person. It is not possible for someone else to have the same loves and hates and lusts and fears and anxieties and hopes and desires as you yourself have. You are unique, you are yourself and there never has been, or can be, someone who is just like you, or who fills your place in the world. And if religion is, as it claims to be, a personal relationship with God, your relationship with God will be something unique to yourself and him. You can listen to preachers preaching, you can read about religion – and probably ought to do so because we can learn from each other's experience – but in the last resort your religion and your prayer is something of your own self. Finally, at the end of your life, you will stand before the judgement seat by yourself. You are responsible for yourself. Many people have contributed towards your goodness and your badness. Many of them may well be blamed and have some responsibility for what is in you, but in the last resort, you are *you* and no one can take your place.

There is an old catechism which proclaims that 'God *made me* for himself, to know him, to love him and to serve him and to be with him for ever in heaven'. I think that this is well worth considering. We all know the processes of human procreation and birth and yet I still believe that God made me and that there was some purpose in this particular joining together of sperm and ovum. When you were born you represented a new hope for the human race. It is as though God, whose power is illimitable, will still refuse his power to make a perfect human being. He leaves it to men to make themselves into human beings. He himself became the prototype. Jesus is man as he is meant to be and we are all potentially men. We may grow to man's estate or we may revert almost to the animal. We may refuse to enter into our heritage. But that you, when you were conceived, represented a unique hope, a unique purpose, is to my mind clear.

Then the old catechism says that you were made by God *for himself*. You were not made by God for your parents or for your employer or for success or failure or for anything or anybody. You were made by God for himself. In other words, with all the myriads of failures that there have been in mankind, he hoped that you, and even I when I was conceived, would be the kind of person who would know him and love him and serve him at any cost. I know that I have failed and have not done this. And you, if you are honest, will probably admit the same: that you have not been what you were, and indeed are, meant to be.

Of course, this does not mean that we are not meant to be involved in the world and to make our lives in the world as creative in every possible way as we can. This again is one of the basic paradoxes of life and I can only go on saying what I shall inevitably repeat again and again in this book, that the more one is involved in the world and its affairs, the more one needs to be involved in God. And the more one is truly involved in God, the more one is forced to be involved in the affairs of the world. This is the paradox of the Church and she must learn to live with it as each one of us has to learn to live with ourselves. The Christian is meant to live with both truths, with feet firmly planted in both worlds. We are wholly God's, God's creatures, made in the image of God. *But* 'God so loved the *world*, that he gave . . .' We must love what he loved, so we must wholly love the world. That is our vocation. I am particularly conscious of this myself because I have so often been accused of being a 'political priest' – that is, of interfering in controversial matters of human welfare when I should be concentrating on the supernatural. Of course I ought to be as wholly involved in God as I can possibly be, but I know that I must also be wholly involved in this world and it is just not possible to be involved in this world without becoming involved in politics. After all, the word 'politics' comes from the Greek for 'citizenship' and, whether they like it or not, Christians are citizens of some particular country. even though, as St Paul says, it is not a lasting citizenship and they also seek the city which is to come.

Of course this 'dual nationality' is extraordinarily difficult in practice. The world is so immediate, so over-whelming and surrounding. But then so is God. 'In him we live, and move, and have our being.' He is closer to me 'than breathing, and nearer than hands and feet'. The more insistent and urgent the world becomes, and the more it pulls, the more we need to plunge ourselves into God – *not* in order to escape from the world but so that we may live to the full in the world, live exuberantly and confidently instead of just existing. 'I am come that they might have life, and that they might have it more abun-dantly.' And we are called to bring that life into the world – into business and politics, into dying and being born, into games and dancing and parties, into every single thing that we do. This kind of life means living in love and it is like what happens when one is in love. There is utter trust and relaxation and confidence, a new awareness and a new look at everything – a new vitality. It is the result of being in love with God.

Another way of thinking about what feels to us like a divided loyalty is to try and realize that in fact there is no clear dividing line between the natural and the super-natural. One can only draw a line between God on the one hand and every other created being on the other. It does not matter whether these beings are purely spiritual, like the angels and archangels, or human beings like ourselves, or whether they are the simplest forms of creation –

plants and inanimate objects. We all have our creature-liness in common because we have all been created.

The word 'supernatural' simply means something which is superlatively natural, just as in slang use we talk of a 'super' experience or a 'super' car, meaning a most wonderful experience or a most magnificent car. When we human beings reach out towards God and are vouch-safed some glimpses of his being, this is a supernatural experience because then we are being most natural, we are being ourselves at our very best, and so we become more truly human. And the reverse is of course true – if we do not reach out and up, we become subhuman and eventually, it seems, are likely to become extinct.

Teilhard de Chardin was a distinguished palaeontologist (which means an expert in extinct species), as well as being a Roman Catholic priest. So he ought to have known what he was talking about when he said 'the day is not far distant when humanity will realize that biologically it is face to face with the choice between suicide and adoration'. I can't help feeling that he was rather sticking his neck out to use the word 'biologically' in this context but, as I understand it, he means that unless we go on developing the supernatural side of our nature, our capa-city for God, as once we developed our capacity to think and speak and use our hands, we will get stuck as the dinosaurs got stuck. We will be yet another species which failed to meet the challenge of evolution and so died out.

But whether or not it is *biologically* true that man must adore or perish, it is certainly true theologically and psychologically. Adoration comes from the Latin 'ad-orare', 'praying towards' – reaching out to that which is beyond ourselves. It is the beginning and the climax of love, and especially of the self-abandonment in growing, deepening trust which is a vital part of any love, human or divine. It contains deep thanksgiving and penitence, and aware-ness that, whatever happens, it's really all right. 'All manner of thing shall be well', as Julian of Norwich says. It begins with glimpses of God, not only in prayer but also in nature, in art and music or a great building, and in our love and trust for each other, and it grows in an ever-deepening awareness that all things reflect the glory of God. As we stretch out, lean out to the glory and learn to adore, we grow in stature and know that we are growing more aware, more human, more real, more encouraged in the best sense of that word. It is the highest function of mankind and one which we share with the angels. And if we do not turn outwards and upwards to adore, we turn in on ourselves, and this is damaging in the plainest physical terms. Most of our heart-attacks and ulcers and other psychosomatic troubles come because our minds and hearts are focused on ourselves. 'It all depends on *me.*' 'It's *my* fault, *my* responsibility, *my* business', and so of course we become frenetic and anxious and depressed. Making little gods of ourselves and our own achievements, or of any other human being, is a short road to death.

CHAPTER THREE

The glory that is 'God'

Up to this point, I have begged the question of what I mean by 'God'. A great many people beg this question throughout their lives, and go on saying that they do or don't 'believe' in God when they have not got the faintest notion what they mean by the word. I often wish we could scrap it altogether and use 'Om' or something instead.

To some people the word 'God' is just an expletive or a swear-word – an explosive religious noise with no real content at all. To others it means a sort of supreme schoolmaster with an all-seeing eye and exceptionally severe punishments for cutting chapel, undone homework and 'having a go' with the gardener's daughter behind the bicycle shed. The current reaction against this particular image has been to deny personality to God at all and think of him as some sort of 'it' – as a source of energy, a first cause behind the universe, grinding out our destiny regardless of our needs and loves and fears, or else, at the other extreme, as 'the ground of our being', with no real identity at all apart from ourselves. Many nice, sincere Christians have a vague image of someone rather like a large fierce dog – the sort of animal which might be dangerous and which people edge round nervously, saying, 'Nice dog, good dog', in ingratiating tones. They try to stroke and pacify God in exactly the same way because they think that God wants nice things said to him in order to keep him in a good temper. (This is a confusion which has arisen from our need to praise, which is quite a different matter.)

God does not need to be praised or pacified. He does not need anything. He is Existence and Being, who not only created but eternally holds all things in life – there is no existence apart from him. He is all in all. We call him personal because that is the highest category of being which we can know, but he is personal in a way infinitely beyond our experience or our capacity to comprehend. He is love – love perfectly fulfilled within the one being of Father, Son and Holy Spirit. He needs nothing from man at all; but he does desire us. He desires us to share in his life and love. He has made us to share in it in so far as we are capable of doing so, and it is this prospect of sharing in perfect life and love and liberty and joy that makes the great scholars and mystics who have spent a lifetime in worship run out of words when they are trying to say what 'God' means to them. St Thomas Aquinas, for instance, at the end of his vast, many-volumed work, the *Summa Theologica*, finally says that he must lay down his pen because there are no words for what he wants to say.

Archbishop Clayton of Cape Town said to me once, 'If you cannot put a thing into words, you do not really know what you mean', and this is very often true. But when it comes to talking about the great experiences of life, even as ordinary an experience as human love, I think it is valid to say that there are no words which can fully express them. Art, music and poetry are all attempts to search into and express the inexhaustible mystery of reality – of the meaning of life and our experience. They stretch out to what is always beyond our reach, to that which is hidden.

The centre of all mystery is God himself. He is beyond. His being is most secret. He has been called 'the unutterable beauty'. He hides himself. As the Psalmist says, 'He hath made clouds and thick darkness to cover him'. He does not hide because he wants to, for God is love and love desires to reveal himself, to open himself, to give himself, but we are limited and human, not able fully to comprehend. So he remains, in the true meaning of the Greek word, a mystery, something so utterly beyond our understanding that we *cannot* talk about it or describe it.

Mostly we have to use negative words to try and describe God – we say that he is non-finite, non-changing, not bound by time, and so on, because the positive words are so much too small. But, even so, many of the things we say about him sound impossible, contradictory, and this is of course inevitable, because if there is any truth at all in what I have called 'God', he is the truth and the resolution at the heart of all the paradoxes. He is so utterly beyond any possible comprehension by our finite minds that we have to stand in one position, as it were, to see one aspect of him and then turn around and try to glimpse him from another aspect. God is infinite and so there are an infinite number of ways of experiencing him, and each one of them, provided it is a true experience, is part of the one great glorious truth.

Happily, we are told in the Bible not to try to know or understand God but to love him, with all our heart and mind and soul and strength. The mind comes into it, certainly, but not the mind alone. (The Athanasian creed is a beautiful but chilling example of what happens if you try to use pure intellect to comprehend the nature of the Godhead.) We cannot even describe another human in purely intellectual terms and get over an idea of their real nature. We can only say what we know *about* him or her, and so we come back to the greatest of all texts, 'God is love'. We cannot picture love, but we can learn about it, think about it, consider it. More importantly, we can experience love and practise it, and if we are considering love, we are considering God.

There are no words that can express the love of God and yet that love must be expressed. Christians believe that it *is* expressed in Jesus, and in that sense Jesus is 'the Word' – the only perfect expression of the love of God. And lest that Word be lost, misinterpreted, misheard or misunderstood, it is embodied in flesh, there to be recognized through all eternity.

'The Word was made flesh, and dwelt among us.' That is how John opens his gospel. Just the stark, staring fact. He doesn't argue it, he just proclaims it. God became man in the body of a woman, became man with a human heart to live a human life. Jesus is the ultimate paradox and the means by which all our contradictions may be reconciled. He is truly God. 'God of God, Light of Light, very God of very God, begotten, not made [as *we* have been made or created], being of one substance with the Father, by whom all things were made', as the Creed expresses it, in language which almost bursts with the strain of using finite words to express the infinite. But he is also truly man. He is not a mixture of the two – something in between – he is not some sort of fairy or angel or anything of that kind. He is God *and* man and it is upon that glorious, unimaginable fact and upon the personal experience of meeting and knowing him, that the Christian faith rests. It has no other basis. Jesus is *the* person, love embodied in man, and he is the centre of all things. That is what he claims for himself. 'Come unto me . . . and I will give you rest.' 'No man cometh unto the Father, but by me.' 'I am the way, the truth, and the life.' 'I am the light of the world.'

Nowadays, it seems to me, we water down not only his divine nature but his human nature as well. People have got so used to the airy-fairy sentimental slop which they were told about Jesus as children and which has got all mixed up with the festival of Christmas that they forget what his real life and death were like.

The first Christmas night must have been anything but the silent, holy time which the carols go on about. Jews from all over the country had been forced to come to Bethlehem for the census and we know that the town was crammed so full that Joseph could find no room even for a woman in labour. There would have been soldiers on the lookout for trouble from the chronically rebellious Jews, civil servants, street traders, hucksters, sneak thieves, and the rest, all shouting, squabbling and cursing – anything but a silent night.

So, in desperation, Mary was pushed into a stable to collapse on to the stinking straw and bear her child – a child, remember, who had been conceived well before marriage, as everyone in her home village must have known. Joseph had accepted the baby, but few people who knew Joseph could have believed he was responsible. He must have endured a lot of sneers and titters for taking 'second-hand goods' and allowing someone else's brat to be foisted on him because he was so besotted about young Mary. And what Mary must have gone through (and Jesus too, as a child and a young man) can only be imagined. Certainly Jesus was referred to as 'Mary's son' all through his life.

It was not much of a beginning, and it did not get better by any ordinary standards. Jesus lived a totally obscure existence in an obscure dump of a hill village until he was nearly thirty years old and then he started wandering round the country, being extremely rude about the 'establishment' of his time and collecting around him a bunch of tax-gatherers (who had toadied to the Romans in return for the right to fleece their own people), prostitutes, beggars, lepers, anyone and everyone except the respectable, devout 'church people' of the time. He had much more in common with the hippies than most of us like to realize.

After about three years of this, his followers realized that they were not going to get much out of it and they dwindled to a handful of hangers-on. No one much cared when he was arrested, condemned by a bit of a fiddle, and put to death by slow torture. Why should anyone bother? Hundreds of men were crucified by the Romans in Palestine every year.

These are the facts about Jesus' life and death and they have precious little to do with the reindeer and old gentleman in cotton-wool and red dressing-gown which we get at the celebration of his birth, or with the soulful-looking sexless being in a white nightie, surrounded by impossibly angelic-looking children, which most of us were shown pictures of in Sunday school.

There are other facts: the power which Jesus exercised over the minds and bodies of men; his unnerving skill in going to the heart of things whenever he was challenged or questioned; his demand for total self-giving from those who seek the kingdom of heaven; his deliberate refusal of the way of power and his taking of the way of love regardless of the cost; the glorious victory of his death and the mystery of the empty tomb. And then there is the fact that those who followed him to the end and who should have been slinking off home feeling utter fools and glad to be out of it all with whole skins, instead were filled with glorious, bursting incredulous joy, and shouted to the world that he was not dead but living and that they had seen and touched him. It is also a fact that this transformation was not something which happened only to the first disciples. Millions of people from that day to this (including myself) have claimed that they have encountered the risen Christ, and that their lives have been changed as a result. Certainly there can be no dispute that their lives have changed.

The fact that Jesus was truly God was not immediately obvious even to those who lived closest to him. It began to become clear after the great events of his life, death, resurrection and ascension were completed, but even then hundreds of years passed before this belief was formulated in the words of the Creed which we use in church today. Those words are an attempt to sum up the facts of Christian experience – and personal experiences, especially of love, are by their nature impossible to express properly in words. They just exist, and the more you experience them, the more true you know them to be. The statements in the Creed are likely to seem literally a non-sense to an agnostic enquirer who is brought flat up against the articles in the Creed and does not try to stretch out further. But when we begin to experience and reach out, however blindly, to all that the life and death and resurrection of Jesus means, it no longer matters that we cannot know *how* the incarnation happened. It is just something that we *know*. John Austin Baker finally concludes in his great book, *The Foolishness of God*: 'It is absurd, it cannot possibly be true, but deep down inside there is no question about it. The Cross is not a picture of God. This was God himself.'[1]

In the end, that is something which each of us has to experience for himself, and if it takes a lifetime to come to the point where one can say 'I believe' with total conviction – well, that does not matter. What does matter is that we are honest in our search, not evading the difficult questions but also not evading the challenge of faith when it meets us.

I cannot adequately put into words my experience of God the Father and God the Son, but I find it harder still to talk about the third person of Divine Being, the Holy Spirit. I myself have always preferred to call him 'the Lord the Spirit'. He *is* the Lord, the 'giver of life', who 'moved upon the face of the waters' at the beginning of time and brought order and life from chaos, and he continues to be the sustaining breath of life in its fullest sense to every living creature on this earth. But to Christians the Holy Spirit is more than this. Jesus, we are told, was conceived 'by the Holy Ghost of the Virgin Mary', and whatever we may understand by this, it is certain that a new *kind* of life came into the world from that moment. 'I am come that they might have life, and that they might have it more abundantly', said Jesus, and that promise was kept. It is not a rarefied, spiritual, saint-in-a-stained-glass-window sort of life either. The first recorded comment on the Church and on Christians was that they must be a

[1] This is part of a personal statement at the end of the book and I find it deeply moving and convincing as the culmination of an honest and scholarly attempt to look at the historical Christ. The quotation comes on page 408 of the book which was published by Darton, Longman & Todd in 1970, and in Fontana in 1975.

bunch of drunks, obviously half-seas-over, and at nine o'clock in the morning too! Not the sodden, wounded, tragic drunks that we see around the London streets, but sizzling, fizzing, bubbling over with love and life and laughter, praising God in all sorts of strange tongues because their own language just wasn't enough, having a hilarious time, and not caring what anyone thought about it. That is the work of the Spirit, bringing life abundant, and if you want to know why it doesn't happen today, the answer is that it does. All over the world, men and women of every denomination from Roman Catholic to extreme Evangelical are again receiving this outpouring of the Spirit with all the fullness of joy and of mental and physical healing, as well as the gift of speaking in tongues and proclaiming the faith, that the first Christians had.

I have not received the Spirit in this particular way myself. In fact I have only once experienced him as a power from outside myself, rather than as a living, growing force within me. That happened, as I have already described in *Encountering Darkness*, when I was still a layman, on a hot, still, Christmas Eve. I went to midnight Mass in Johannesburg Cathedral and as I knelt at the altar-rail I felt a breeze, a draught, a wind strong and cooling, blowing over me. That one encounter was wholly sufficient to convince me of his existence as a person but I myself have had no other Pentecostal experience.

I am not anxious or disturbed about this. I do not mean that I am satisfied with myself, but I do know that there are very many great Christians of all ages who have not had a 'Pentecostal' experience so it is perfectly possible to be a Christian both with it and without it. The power to begin living in the new life of the Spirit is in fact given to us when we are baptized in the name of the Father, the Son and the Holy Spirit and he mediates and makes active the power and love of God within each one of us who is Christian. For the Holy Spirit is the lord and giver of love as well as life. He 'proceedeth from the Father

and the Son' – and how I loathe the word 'proceedeth'!
He doesn't 'proceed'. He comes *pouring* out – he is a
torrent of love, like the Niagara Falls, cascading between
the Father and the Son and then flooding out and on
towards us. 'The love of God is shed abroad in our hearts
by the Holy Ghost which is given unto us.'

This of course brings us slap up against 'the doctrine of
the Trinity', which is such a stumbling-block to so many
people. It is not in fact a doctrine at all. As Dr Mascall
points out in *The Christian Universe*, 'there is a doctrine
about the Trinity, as there are doctrines about many other
facts of existence, but, if Christianity is true, the Trinity
is not a doctrine; the Trinity is God.'[2]

There have been many attempts to teach the nature of
the Holy Trinity and many books written about it, but I
am not capable of such undertakings and in any case
this is not the place for it. Reason and intellect cannot
express the mystery because words fall utterly short, and
any attempt to use analogies to grasp it – such as the three-
leafed shamrock – are more disastrous still. The Trinity
is the Being of God and is quite beyond any imaginative
analogies. The imagination just boggles at the idea of
'three in one'. In any case, it is never true to say that God
is 'three in one'. We can say that he is three *persons* in
one God, if that helps, but it is still hopelessly limited
language. We use the word 'persons' when we refer to
God because a person is capable of knowing and forgiving,
of loving and being loved, and it is the highest category
of being which we have experienced. But we have got to
keep very sharply and deeply cut into our minds the
realization that when we use the word 'person' as a
description of the nature of the Godhead we are using an
expression which is wholly, totally and completely inadequate. He is utterly beyond, he is utterly other. He is
far greater than anything which the words 'person' or
'personality' can convey.

2 *The Christian Universe* (Darton, Longman & Todd, London, 1966),
p. 51.

The same is true of the words 'Father, Son and Holy Spirit' when we use them to try and convey the nature of God. They are hopelessly inadequate images, but we have no better ones and Jesus himself taught us to use them. He spoke of himself as the Son. He promised us the Spirit of truth and he taught us to call God 'Father'. I believe that he taught us to use this word partly because man is at his best in his own fatherhood and so we are reaching out towards something of which fatherhood is merely the tiniest glimpse. The true father, in our own imagination, is the begetter, the lover, the one who guards and cares and cherishes, and so fatherhood, which is the highest category of our own experience, comes nearest to the lowest possible concept of God.

When I started to be a Christian I had no knowledge of 'the doctrine of the Trinity' at all. I knew that there was such a doctrine and because I was so utterly lost I was prepared to give it what little acquiescence I could. I knew that it was embedded in the Creed and that the great saints and scholars of the Church considered it to be of the essence of the Christian faith, so although I couldn't see a great deal of sense in it, I wasn't prepared to argue. I thought then, as I think now, that a great many people know a lot more about this sort of thing than I do.

Many people may have to start where I started and just go on from there. It is certain that the disciples who followed Jesus had no concept of the Trinity. They knew that Jesus talked of his Father, but it wasn't until long after his death and resurrection that they realized the unity between the Father and the Son, and it was certainly many years after the experience of the coming of the Lord the Spirit at Pentecost that the idea of the Trinity began to form itself. The history of the early Church is simply one of hammering out, as it were, the truth of this great doctrine, and it took three or four hundred years before it was finally proclaimed as being as close to the truth as the Church can get.

As I have lived the Christian life I have come more and

more to realize that the doctrine of the Trinity *does* reveal the truth, even if it is the lowest, most basic kind of truth, about the nature and existence of God. It does now seem possible that when I am capable – perhaps long after this life is over – I shall see how pale a reflection of the true nature of God the doctrine of the Trinity is.

I have only once really 'experienced' the Trinity and that was, as these things usually are for me, through the Mass (about which I talk later in this book). The experience was quite unexpected. I was making no particular attempt to meditate or think about the Trinity, but I suddenly saw that the Mass is in fact the Trinity of love at work. It is Jesus, the only begotten Son of God, offering his life to the Father on behalf of all his children. And the whole action is, as it were, mediated by the Lord the Spirit, who is the Lord, the giver of life, so that the Mass is simply the triune God as he reveals himself at his work of love on earth. I cannot convey what this experience meant to me because personal glimpses of love and loveliness are impossible to describe in words. All I can say is that this happened, and since then the triune nature of love has been a reality for me. But this kind of experience is something which God himself gives us when we are ready for it, and we cannot make it happen by ourselves. As I say so often in this book, the important thing is to get started from where you are, and if you find the doctrine of the Trinity is a stumbling-block, just say so in your prayers. But do also try and reach out in the hope that, as so many other Christians have done before you, you yourself may come at some time to a knowledge of him as three persons in one God.

CHAPTER FOUR

Response

I have talked at length about the divided, paradoxical nature of man and about the mystery of God and about my utter belief and experience that we cannot find joy or peace or wholeness unless we somehow stretch out in longing to that source of love and healing which is beyond ourselves. Such stretching out is the beginning of faith and love. It is also the beginning of 'religion' because it is in essence the search for a relationship with a God and 'religion' means a bond or binding together and therefore a relationship.

We can only start, if we decide to start at all, from where we happen to be. I began myself with a complete dissatisfaction with life as it was and myself as I was and, somewhere in the pit of my stomach, a belief, or if not a belief, then a desire, that there is, or should be, somewhere, a power and a purpose beyond myself.

I know of some people who have started their religion from utter desperation, more or less the place from which I started, and I know of some who have started through an overplus of joy and wonder and human love and have realized that this was the reflection of something even greater. Quite frankly, I don't care where you start, but start you must and nobody else can do it for you. You have somehow to respond to the desperation, to the joy, to the sorrow, the anxiety, the fear, or whatever possesses you at the moment, and try and reach out through it to whatever reality may be beyond.

This response of the soul (or the self, if you prefer it) to God is what we call prayer. It is, obviously, a wholly

individual thing and no two people do it alike, but it is
only sensible, when wondering how to begin, to look at
what Jesus had to say about it, since he is the greatest
teacher about prayer as he is about everything else to do
with God and man. You may remember that his disciples
came to him and said, 'Lord, teach us to pray.' It was a
curious request because they were devout Jews and must
have been taught to 'say their prayers' from their childhood. But being taught to 'say your prayers' is a very
different thing from being taught how to pray.

These men had seen Jesus at prayer and must have
realized that there was a quality of relationship or intercourse or communication between Jesus and the Father
which was more real than their own experience. At any
rate, they wanted something more deep, more real, than
they already had.

But Jesus did *not*, as is so often implied, tell them to go
and repeat like parrots a rigmarole of words which begins
'Our Father . . .' and has become known as 'the Lord's
Prayer'. In fact he warned them again and again about the
sort of pagan prayer (of which there is far too much in
church and amongst church people today) by which you
believe that if you use a great many 'correct' words you
must be getting somewhere or doing something. It is
possible to repeat 'the Lord's Prayer' quite automatically
without doing any real praying at all.

Jesus said, 'After this manner therefore pray ye' – '*in
this kind of way*'. And he started with the Jewish word
'Abba' – 'Father'. There was nothing very new about
calling God 'Father' – this concept of God was already
well known both to the Jews and to many pagan religions.
But what Jesus did which was rude and irreligious and
shocking was to discard the great 'religious' word of deep
filial awe and respect for the Father of all life, and sub-
stitute for it the Jewish baby word 'Abba'. (He probably
did not say 'which art in heaven'. This is thought to have
been added later by some religious evangelist who felt
that 'Abba' was too intimate and added 'which art in

heaven' in order to put God back where he belonged, 'up there'. In fact heaven is not where God is. Where God is – that's heaven. So if we do say 'which art in heaven', we are not proclaiming the absence of God but the presence of God here with us.)

So Jesus taught us to begin praying by talking to and thinking of God in the same way as a small child would turn to its father. Unfortunately some of us can't get much of a picture of fatherhood from our own fathers but we can all perhaps imagine what we ourselves would most wish to be like as fathers to our own children – all that fatherhood might be in terms of belonging, care, strength, comfort – and that's what 'Abba' means.

All words matter. Words and life belong to each other. And the most important words are the words of response. Our first words as children are a response – mainly to our mothers. And later there is the response of the lover and the beloved. Such words are probably not many in number but their meaning grows as we use them in depth and richness and love. And Jesus tells us to respond to God by saying 'Father'. We may say it in an agonized cry of desperation or with affection and love and thanksgiving, but it is the most basic of man's words before God, and if we can say it and mean it, then the whole of life takes on a different perspective. Love and joy, or pain and loneliness, whatever grief or separation you may have, it all happens within the fatherhood of God. 'Underneath are the everlasting arms.' Whatever my sin or desperation, if I can say 'Abba, Father', I proclaim that I am a son of God – not a slave or a servant but a *son*, and no behaviour of mine can change that. (That is what the story of the prodigal son is about.) But I remain a son of God because I belong with Jesus, *the* son of God. *With him* I say 'Abba, Father'.

But we cannot develop even an earthly relationship with a parent or child or friend unless we take time to be with the other person and to talk with him alone. One of the themes of the Bible is that God calls us to be alone with him to listen to him. 'When thou prayest, enter into thy closet, and . . . shut thy door.' Get alone, get quiet, get away from all the things that attract you or distract you so much. Come and be alone. And that is what prayer is, amongst other things – being all by yourself with God; face to face – a man and his maker; the lover and the beloved, the child and his father, or however you like to think of it. And then when you are alone, or perhaps together with someone you love and trust and want to share this with, you have to start responding to God from where you are and and who you are – *not* with the sort of thing which you imagine it is 'proper' to talk to God about.

The ideal response to God has been fairly clearly set out by the great writers on prayer throughout the ages. At their simplest they say this : If I was suddenly to be able to see God revealed in all his glory, my first response would inevitably be one of utter awestruck wonder – the kind of breathless, speechless wonder of a small child taken into a darkened room on Christmas Eve and shown the Christmas lights burning on the tree. So if we could see God, our first response would be adoration. The feeling that would next come to me would be one of abject horror of myself as compared with the great glory of love sweeping down towards me, so that my second reaction would be that of contrition or penitence, sorrow for my sins and all my sinfulnesses. Then, ideally, I would realize that God still loved me in spite of these, so I would go on to thanksgiving for all that God had done for me in spite of the awful things that I had done to him, and finally I would go on to supplication, to plead for God's help for me and those whom I love. So those are the four main aspects of prayer – adoration, contrition, thanksgiving and supplication.

But I do not think that for most of us it happens just like that because obviously we do *not* see God revealed in all his glory. Our eyes are, perhaps mercifully, too blind, and although we can learn to see the divine glory reflected in earthly things, we all see it differently. An engineer or a mathematician may have an idea of love-liness quite different from that of a farmer or gardener. A young lover perhaps will conceive of glorious beauty through his experience of his girl's body and the joy of their relationship together.

It doesn't matter where you start from. You are God's person and so you stand where you are and try to reach out from there, always being as honest with yourself as you possibly can be – and that is a very difficult thing to do.

It is important not to try to put on any acts and it is important to try and be your own self because it is *you* whom God loves, not some false personality which you are trying to put on for his benefit. He may not *like* you very much as you are, but he *loves* you and wants you to become something other than you are. This will only begin to happen as you begin to respond to him with the real part of yourself.

I know that when I began to want to be a Christian my first words were, 'If there is a God, this is what I want to say . . .', and I talked of myself and my life and my hopes and fears and then I tried to talk about him and what I thought he might be, and be able to do. I think it was all very jejune, but it was at least honest and I know of no other way in which to begin. But almost immediately I found that I had to get hold of some books on prayer (of which there are very many) and try to learn to get some more order into my response to God.

Many people start with an overflowing sense of thank-fulness for human love and friendship, for food and health and strength, for books and letters and all sorts of lovely things. Other people experience a tremendous conviction of sin, suddenly realizing, perhaps through some very obvious sin in which they have been discovered, just how degraded they have become, and so they may well start from penitence. Others have started their prayer because they or someone they love has a desperate need for release from pain or terror or some danger which is beyond human control. As I say, I think you can start anywhere you like, and then gradually you have to work at bringing in the other aspects of prayer which don't come quite so naturally to you. You have to practise them as you have to practise five-finger exercises so that you can begin to grow in a true response to God. Sometimes adoration will not come for a long, long time but even so I think it is a good thing to practise it. There are books of prayers, such as *My God, My Glory* by E. Milner-White, and many other writings, including the great prayers of the Psalms, which proclaim the glory of God and are valuable exercises to use. It is not hypocritical to use these words even though one doesn't mean them whole-heartedly. I know that if I am going to progress in prayer I have got to stretch out towards adoration, and the only way in which I can do this is by practising. After all, no great pianist ever becomes able to play a great piece of music or to compose music freely until he has by slogging hard at exercises and constant practice got to such a pitch that composition or magnificent playing begins to come naturally to him. It is exactly the same with prayer.

If you are honestly trying to begin to stretch out to God in this way, you will find, perhaps to your surprise, that you are beginning to love him. It is not in fact surprising because even on a human level it is impossible to begin to know someone who is worthwhile without beginning to love him or her. And so one presses forward into love, not urgently but with longing. In this particular connection, I always think of St Teresa's prayer. She said, 'Oh God, I do not love thee. Oh my God, I do not want to love thee. But, oh my dear God, I do *want* to want to love thee.' And this, I suppose, is mostly where the love of God begins, with a desire to want to love him. Very often it is a selfish desire, because we know, at least subconsciously, that we can never be our true selves except in relationship to him. To grow to adulthood means to love God. Unless we love him, we slowly begin to lose our humanity and to die. We exist to love and to be loved by God and without him we are not human.

One thing we do know for certain is that this knowledge and love cannot grow without real disciplined effort on our part. I think that this is where many people's religion breaks down. They go to church and try to be helpful and kindly to their neighbours but they make no disciplined attempt to know God in any real sense and therefore loving him seems impossible, and ultimately serving him is impossible too.

So I believe it is completely essential if you mean to get anywhere in the Christian life to put aside some specific time for this exercise. I should say that the very barest possible minimum is a quarter of an hour in a day but this should very soon grow to a minimum of half an hour. As to when and where prayer should be made, this again is a matter which every individual should decide for himself. Ideally the early morning is the best time. If you make your main prayer at night you will probably be too tired and too full of the events of the day to be fully capable of responding whole-heartedly to God, and for me at least, kneeling beside my bed at night is much too conducive to going to sleep there and then.

Some people get worried about the 'right' posture for prayer. The most natural position for most Western people does seem to be on their knees although in later years I myself have begun to find it easier (and I am not sure that easiness is the right criterion) to pray sitting down. I have also tried praying standing up with arms outstretched and this is sometimes valuable. Some people sit cross-legged or on their heels. The kind of posture does not really matter at all. What matters is that it is a position in which you can pray.

Most writers on prayer say that the right way to start is by recollection. This simply means that I have been dissipated (that is, fragmented) by my response to all sorts of people and things and I need to collect myself together into one person, into myself, so that the whole of myself can begin to turn towards God and respond to him. Some people do this recollection by reading a passage from the Bible. Others look at a crucifix or a picture or repeat a particular phrase, and I would advise you to experiment with all these methods. My own personal habit is taken from the Eastern mystics. I find it very valuable to sit or kneel and take about ten very deep breaths (not gasps) right down into my stomach, into the centre of my being, while I try to identify myself with the whole of God's creation; the whole of creation breathes, as it were, and I am a part of it. The Spirit of God moved over the face of the waters and brought cosmos out of chaos and so I breathe in the Lord the Spirit; I put myself under another Pentecost so that the breath of God may enter into my being and calm and collect me.

Then, because I am such an unrecollected and dissipated person, I find it almost essential to have with me a pencil and paper because almost as soon as I start to pray all sorts of other things enter into my mind. Some of them I ought to try to discard if I can, but many of them are things which may well be of practical value. Often as I begin my prayers I realize that I haven't visited Mr and Mrs So-and-so for some time, so I make a note of it on my bit of paper and then I can get on with my prayer. Very often at the end of my prayer time I have all sorts of notes. They may be ideas for sermons, for further prayer, or reminders about remembering to buy petrol or sausages. I find this much less distracting than saying to myself, 'I mustn't be thinking about sausages when I am saying my prayers, *but* I simply must not forget the sausages.' Once I get the word 'sausages' written down on the bit of paper they are out of the way and the prayer goes more easily.

This is not a book specifically about prayer and I don't want to go on and on about it, but I think it is worth saying that as you read about prayer you will find that most of the writers divide the life of prayer into three stages. They use various names but normally they talk about vocal prayer, mental prayer and contemplative prayer or something of this kind. I think that the less notice you take of this the better, although you certainly ought to be aware that there are different kinds of prayer.

Vocal prayer is fairly easy to understand. It is the prayer in which we do a lot of the talking. Mental prayer is where we mostly do the listening, and contemplative prayer is something of which I have so little experience that I can hardly speak of it, except to say that it is a satisfying kind of prayer. There doesn't seem to be much in the way of words on either side but it is just a joy in communication. My own experience is that prayer, rather than being a sort of ladder up which one progresses laboriously through these different stages, resembles much more a spiral in which one comes back and back again to the same point but each time at a rather higher (or deeper) and more satisfying level than the time before. All of this you need to try out for yourself.

Most people begin to learn mental prayer by practising some sort of meditation – that is, with a conscious effort to listen to what God has to say to them. Often they begin this by reading a short passage from the Bible and considering what Jesus is saying to them in their own particular situation through these words. (The imagination is a strong part of our own mental make-up, so it is a good thing to form a picture of Jesus saying these words or of what the words themselves are saying so that our minds don't wander and we can listen.) But it is also perfectly possible to meditate, that is, to listen to God, by looking at a picture, listening to music, or in many other ways.

Some people just cannot meditate in this way and certainly meditation is only one of the entrances to mental prayer or 'colloquy' with God. This means that a few words are, as it were, thrown up to God and returned to us with a deeper meaning and a greater warmth.

Very often they are words which we repeat over and over again, just as we do in human love. The words may be the name of Jesus himself, or they may be any other words or sentences which we have heard or read and into which we want to enter more deeply. We keep such words in our mind and seek and search and wait, not anxiously, not hysterically banging on the door for an answer, but remembering what Jesus himself says: 'Seek, and ye shall find; knock, and it shall be opened unto you' – all of which are gentle expressions. It may well be that very soon indeed the beginnings of contemplative prayer, that is to say, satisfaction in the utterance of no word at all, will be given. Sometimes reaching this sort of prayer means really hard work, but it should never be made with anxiety or in desperation.

One of the best known facts about the life of prayer is that there are times of aridity or dryness and these are necessary for growth. If we found ordinary vocal prayer becoming absolutely real and we were able to stay satisfied with that, we would never advance any further. If we are to press forward, God must *seem* to withdraw from us, just as a father teaching his child to walk has to take his hand away or the child will never learn to walk by himself. And as soon as his hand is taken away the child will probably come down with a bump, as you and I often do in our lives of prayer. But this is the signal for going forward, not for giving up. It is simply a sign that God is calling us into a closer, deeper relationship with him, and so it is wholly essential to press forward through these times when prayer seems meaningless and one begins to wonder whether the whole thing hasn't been a mistake. It is at these times that I personally find books of prayers most valuable, because I can take other people's prayers on my lips and *want* to mean them although I may feel that I do not in fact mean them. I am simply determined that I am going to grow in stature and so I am going to go on seeking God. I know that he loves me and that he is not able to forsake me and that if I persevere I shall know his closeness once again.

Just how intercession works, I have no idea at all, but Jesus certainly taught us to pray for things and told us

that those prayers would be answered. It is a fact of my
own experience that if I am conducting a mission in a
parish and there are a considerable number of people who
are at that time seeking Jesus, keenly intent on trying to
commit themselves more deeply, their prayers for a sick
person seem to produce more noticeable cures than when
a rather long list of names is formally read out at an
ordinary parish service. I can only deduce from this that
the effectiveness of intercession to some extent depends
not on mentioning names but on the keenness of the desire
that God's will should be done. It is basic to remember
that God's will is always loving. I do not believe it is ever
true to say, for instance, that it is God's will that a child
should be run over by a bus. I do not believe it can be
anything of the kind. God must desire to see his children
grow. But there are powers of evil active in the world
and there are so few of us who desire that the will of
God, of love, should be triumphant, that in individual
cases God's will is not done and it is the fault of the sin
of the whole world that this is so. This brings up the
whole problem of evil, and although I cannot deal with
it adequately in a small book like this, I do try to talk
about it further in the next chapter.

Here I only want to emphasize that intercession of any
kind is setting ourselves alongside God against the powers
of evil – against all deadness and disintegration and despair
– and like all coming to grips with evil it is bound to be
costly if it is to be effective. The cross shows us that the
cutting edge of prayer lies in sacrifice. If I really mean
that I offer my prayer 'through Jesus Christ our Lord', I
am talking about the cross, and it isn't much good talking
about the cross unless I am doing something about the
cross. So I believe it to be true that if I am really praying
for somebody I must accompany that prayer by some
personal sacrifice of fasting or discipline or at the least
by a really concentrated urgent effort to be 'with' the
person I am praying for, and, as it were, offer myself as
a channel through which the love and power of God can

pour into and around him.

Equally, it is not much good praying for someone if I am neglecting to do something practical about the situation when it is in my power to do so. Many people think of prayer as some kind of escape from action. 'I'll pray about it' all too often means that you don't intend to do anything else about it (and the chances are that you don't intend to pray really sacrificially about it either). The fact is that true prayer clears our vision and sensitizes our consciences so that the more we pray, the more we find that demands are being made on our love and obedience to go and do things in our daily life – perhaps to stand out against some dishonesty or fiddling, or to take trouble to get to know someone who is unpopular, or to give up time in some way. Whatever it may be, prayer *always* leads to greater involvement with the world, and the more you are involved in the world's affairs, the more danger you are in of being entangled by them and diminished or degraded by their standards and anxieties and pressures. And so, the more you are involved in the world, the more you need to be lifted up again – to be made human again – by your contact with God, by the adoration which I have said is a necessity for truly human existence, and by the knowledge that you are not struggling alone and unsupported against the pain and evil of the world.

Prayer is, of course, like everything else to do with human beings, paradoxical. I have emphasized here the absolute necessity of having time alone in which to know and love God because I think that this *is* essential and it gets too easily pushed aside nowadays. I have little patience with people who come to me and say, 'I don't have time for prayer but I do pray all day long.' Someone once said, 'There are liars, damn liars, and statisticians', and I would add to that list 'those who claim to pray all day long'. *That* kind of prayer can only come from the love of God warming up a great pool of regular prayer from which a mist, as it were, of continuous loving awareness can rise to God all through the day. It just is not possible to begin to learn what God wants from us in our daily life and work unless we start by opening ourselves to God, drawing deep into ourselves his love, and learning to see the world with his eyes.

Our prayer will always swing between learning to see God in the world and lifting the world up to the mystery and glory and love of God. In the past the Church has emphasized the second aspect too much, which I suppose is why there was such excitement over Michel Quoist's book, *Prayers of Life*.[1] People leapt for it because it made clear that prayer need not be an exotic floating away into the wilderness but could be focused on a £5 note or a pornographic magazine. But perhaps the pendulum has swung a bit too far the other way now and we are forgetting our need to be 'lifted up'.

One group of people who are experts on all of this is the Roman Catholic Order of the Little Brothers and Little Sisters of Jesus. These men and women live in small groups in the poorest and most deprived cities and deserts of the world and endure the same insecurity and poverty and gruelling labour as the people whose lives they are trying to share. They try to 'be Jesus' in those places in the same way as their master lived and worked in Nazareth. But what makes it possible for them to live in these conditions and not be destroyed by them is the hour of silent adoration which each Sister and Brother offers every day. They are specifically told not to pray for people or meditate in this time – that has to be done elsewhere. This hour of adoration is a lifting up of themselves to God for his own sake, and it is that and that alone, they say, which makes it possible for them to go down into the depths and give themselves to utter involvement in human life.

But having emphasized the absolute necessity for withdrawal and adoration, I must reiterate that it is of course equally true that God is not only in the place where you go to pray. God just *is*. He permeates and penetrates the whole universe. The supernatural – his presence – is woven

[1] Published by Gill & Son, Dublin, 1963.

into every material thing that there is and we come across him at the most unexpected moments. It may be at a moment of joy or love or fun, or in a sudden certainty that everything is in fact all right. It may be in sorrow or bereavement or fear, or in a flash of awareness when we are doing our ordinary jobs – washing the nappies or bashing a typewriter. The more we try to know God in the silence, the more we will grow in awareness of his presence in our daily lives, and it does not matter where those lives are led. (It was Brother Lawrence, the monastery cook, and not some intellectual choir monk, who wrote one of the great books on this subject, *The Practice of the Presence of God*, and he found God amongst his pots and pans.)

Personally, I find it helpful to try and understand this by comparing God's presence with the radio. If you fiddle with the knobs late at night you get station after station – sometimes modern music or opera, or perhaps a dull talk – but the potentiality of noise and of understanding the noise is always there *provided we are attuned to it*. It is a poor simile really, because the presence of God is much closer than any radio wave. It permeates every fibre of my being. 'Closer is he than breathing, and nearer than hands and feet', and his love upholds our being every second of our lives.

CHAPTER FIVE

The cost of loving

In the last chapter I tried to talk a little about how love between God and God's world can grow from stretching out in prayer. I was not talking about sacrifice but inevitably it crept in (the discipline needed for prayer and the cost of true intercession are both kinds of sacrifice). It crept in because wherever there is love there *must* also be sacrifice. This is because the object of all love is union. The lover and the beloved seek to find union with each other, to become one – and if this is true of human love, it must be much more deeply and profoundly true of divine love.

In an ideal world, love would be a perfect giving and receiving, but we do not live in an ideal world. Even in human love obstacles arise between the lover and the beloved. Sometimes it is through their own fault, sometimes through extraneous circumstances, but once obstacles come between the lover and the beloved, then there is a need for sacrifice. It may be the sacrifice of one's own opinions. It may be the sacrifice of some element of freedom which one treasures. It may be some financial sacrifice. But that sacrifice has to be made before the barrier to union can be overcome.

This is even more true in the love, the relationship, the desire for union, between God and man. That God desires this union between himself and man is proclaimed throughout the whole of the Bible. It is made explicit in Jesus, and on the last night of his life, Jesus put it into words. He prayed 'that they all may be one; as thou, Father, art in me, and I in thee, that they also may be one in us'. And nothing could be a greater proclamation of his desire to be united with us than that.

But as St Teresa says of the union between God and man, this 'is two *different* things becoming one'; and the whole concept of man being united with God is so utterly beyond comprehension that St Teresa goes into a whole paean of joy and delight at the wonder that it might be possible, that these two utterly different things – God the creator, the infinite, the perfect love, and I, the deformed, the sinner, the selfish one – that we should become one. And it can only be done at the most tremendous cost.

In the first instance, if this union is to happen between the perfect God and the sinful man, God must sacrifice himself, must, as it were, give up his glory, lay aside his most transcendent power, in order to provide any common basis on which he and I can meet. So in the Incarnation this is precisely what he does. He lays aside his glory, he is born in the stink of the stable, he associates with man at his most sinful; with man at his most deformed in body and in soul; with the lepers, the publicans, the sinners, the outcast. But of course the final sacrifice is death, and it must be death in its most extreme form, not only the degradation of the death upon the cross, which to the Jew was the ultimate shame, but also the indignity, the trial, the mocking, the crowning with thorns, the scourging, the rejection, denial, betrayal, the human fear in Gethsemane – 'Let this cup pass from me' – the thirst upon the cross, every single possible depth which human beings can reach. This is the kind of sacrifice which God must make if he is to be united with man. And that is precisely what the cross is about. The metaphysics, the theology of it all, has never been understood by anybody, but the practical demonstration is there for the simplest man to see. This is simply love stretching out into the lowest depths to which love can reach. (Had there been any further depths he would have gone to them, and it is indeed recorded that he 'descended into hell', the place of the departed, there to reach out to the souls lost in the unknown blackness which is beyond our comprehension.) The point is simply and clearly made – God is love, and on the cross he demonstrates this to the uttermost.

But of course, it is not only God who has to sacrifice. I must also go to meet him. This is what that phrase, which gets used so glibly, about 'taking up the cross' means. The cross is the symbol of total sacrifice, of the breaking down of obstacles to love at *whatever* cost, and it is just not possible to claim to be a Christian while doing our best to evade the cross. We all do it of course, and sometimes we use a great deal of skill and effort in the process. We dance all round the cross, trying to escape a discipline, a costly decision, a situation where we are going to look fools or whatever it may be. We all see pain and suffering and demands on our patience or time as things to be avoided if we can, whereas if we were truly Christian we would see them as means, voluntary or involuntary, of sacrifice – of setting aside those things in ourselves which are obstacles to love: our prides, our lusts, our fears, our covetousness, our almost everything, because there is so much in us which shuts out love.

Those things in us which are obstacles to love – to union with a beloved – we call 'sin'. Unfortunately, as happens with almost every religious word, the meaning of 'sin' has been badly distorted. It is a common idea that 'sin' is simply the breaking of one of the commandments, and it has often been so far misused as a word as to be equated simply with physical sins such as murder, theft, lust and the like. Of course these are sins, but they are not the deadliest sins of all. Often when we are caught up in one of these traumatic sins which even the world recognizes, we come up against the law of the land, or the common *mores* of a community, and so such sins tend to bring their own punishment upon themselves. For theft and murder we can be imprisoned. For adultery we can be caught with venereal disease or the parenthood of an illegitimate child and if there is a scandal we might lose a job or promotion. But quite apart from their possible consequences, the fact that these sins are so traumatic psychologically very often brings us up against the true nature of what we are doing, and so we turn quickly, if not to repentance, at least to seek for help, for some way out. Very often this means seeking forgiveness either from God or from those whom we have hurt and trying to make a new start.

It seems to me that the really deadly sins are not the obvious wickednesses which make even you and me feel awful but those which creep up on us unawares.

Jesus said, 'Broad is the way that leadeth to destruction.' In other words, the way to destruction is paved with gradually increasing selfishness or prejudice or pride, coldness or lack of generosity, with the little evil growths which form a cancer in ourselves and twist and turn our natures until we become almost inhuman creatures, without ever doing anything which we recognize as being particularly wrong. We just sink gradually downwards.

Many of these unseen, hidden sins are the failure to do something good, rather than actually doing something bad. The sins of omission are the most dangerous of all and Jesus confirmed this when he talked about those souls who would be condemned because 'inasmuch as ye did it not to one of the least of these [my brethren], ye did it not to me'. And in the parable of the talents we are taught that we have to sacrifice our laziness and do the things which need to be done, if we truly wish to grow in love, because the opposite of love has nothing to do with hate; it is not-loving, not-caring. *That* is the pale chilling thing at the centre of man's being. Nothing can be done with you if you don't care, because you yourself have become nothing – non-human – and so you are dead. The Latin for this not-caring is '*acedia*' and it is generally translated into English as 'sloth'. In some ways it is more basic and more deadly than the sin of pride. We all know the symptoms too well in ourselves. 'Well, the world's in a mess but I can't do anything about it.' 'Hunger will kill umpteen million people this year – how will it help if

I give something to save half a dozen of them?' None of us want to see or know the things we can't bear thinking about – and so we go past the Oxfam advertisements or the down-and-outs in the city streets with averted eyes and forget about them as fast as possible. In contrast, the gospels keep saying of Jesus that he was *moved* with compassion. He didn't just say how awful some suffering was, he suffered with the sufferer (which is what compassion means). A more basic translation is 'his bowels yearned' – he had a feeling in the guts as urgent and uncomfortable as gippy tummy and it *moved* – it moved to sacrificial action to break down whatever barriers to love were causing the suffering. We can't all do everything but at least each one of us can do something about one particular agony in the world, and if we do not, that is sin.

Another aspect of sloth is refusing to change. Change is a basic necessity in the Christian life because God himself is immutable. He is changeless, and if his creation is ever to be truly in the image of God and reflect his glory, we must evolve, grow, mature, develop – whatever word one likes to use for change.

Our whole religion is one of movement, and since the capacity for movement means life and its absence is a sure sign of death, the mystery of change is also manifested in the Mass, in that mysterious and wonderful change of the bread and wine into the body and blood of the risen Christ. (I talk about this in the next chapter.)

Sometimes change is gradual – a gentle movement all through an individual – as most growth is. Sometimes God steps in with his might, his bared arm, and grabs an individual as he did Saul on the road to Damascus, calling out a man or a group of men who change the course of the world's history in his name.

But man is a very fearful creature and he does not like the unknown. He hangs on to his security. 'Better the devil you know than the devil you don't know.' Often he tries to escape from any feelings of insecurity by sticking to the habits and customs with which he grew up, quite regardless of whether they are still serving a useful purpose or whether they are now inhibiting further growth. 'That's the way we've always done it so that's the way we shall go on doing it.' In its most extreme form this need for a secure 'thing' which will cope with all the paradoxes and fears and unknowns of life results in some theory or idea or institution becoming enshrined – set up as a god – in place of the God of life and love, and *that* is idolatry.

So, hanging on blindly to a way of believing and being because it makes us feel safe is one of the deadly sins. It sets up a rigid barrier to the love and power of God. It was over the chaos and emptiness of the newly created world that the Spirit of God moved to bring order, cosmos, life. It was from the empty virgin womb of Mary that the new creation, the Lord Jesus, was born, and from the chaos of the crucifixion and the emptiness of the tomb that the fire and wind of the Spirit brought rebirth to man. His power can only act within us if we are ready to open ourselves to change.

Perhaps, after sloth and fear of change, the third commonest and deadliest sin of our generation is trying to have things both ways, to have our cake and eat it. Jesus is quite clear about that. He says, 'Ye cannot serve God and mammon.' And 'mammon' here means not only money but all material possessions. Of course this does not mean that we are not to have possession and enjoy having them, but that is quite different from *serving* them, taking orders from them, letting them dictate what our lives shall be. If we do that, Jesus says, we cannot take orders from God. It just is not possible to have two masters. Most people solve that problem quite easily. They go after possessions, material satisfaction in the widest sense, and leave God alone. But those of us who call ourselves Christians usually have a spiritual squint. One eye is fixed, more or less, on God, looking upwards, and the other is pretty firmly fixed on things, looking downwards. As a result we cannot see our values clearly and so we have divided hearts as well as squinting eyes. All Jesus' promises to his followers in the New Testament were made to those who had gone the whole hog. This is made clear again and again when he says that the kingdom of heaven is like a merchant who sold everything for one pearl or a farmer who sold everything to get a field with treasure in it. Don't look back, don't hesitate and put things off; 'If . . . thine eye be single [fixed on one thing], thy whole body shall be full of light'; and so on and so on. The single eye and undivided heart look to God alone. They watch what he wants and see which way he is pointing and follow it – it is to such men that the kingdom of heaven is promised.

But of course, however hard we try, we *are* uncaring and stick-in-the-mud and double-minded, even if we do not steal, rape or murder. You and I cannot make a perfect act of love because our love is not big enough, not consuming enough, not devouring enough. And so our sin, our barriers, spoil us and separate us, which is what sin always does and what it did pre-eminently on the cross to Jesus. It spoilt his hands and feet with the nails and his head with the crown of thorns and his whole body with the scourging. He had 'no beauty that we should desire him'. He was useless, reduced to the dregs of humanity, and then he was also separated – cut off from the whole source and meaning of his life. To be despised and rejected of men was at least something which had happened often enough before. 'The Son of man hath not where to lay his head.' 'A prophet hath no honour in his own country.' But always before he had had the certainty that God was with him. Men might reject him, but his father would not. And now his father's presence with him was gone and so deep was the horror that Jesus turned from his own native language to the formal Hebrew of the Psalms. 'My God, my God, why hast thou forsaken me?' *And there was no answer*. Remember that when you yourself cry out, 'My God, *why*? Why do you allow this senseless pain, this senseless loss?' There is no real answer that we can understand. The only answer is that it happened on the cross, and the only comfort is that Jesus asked the same question.

We, who habitually do our best to escape from the presence of God, cannot begin to imagine the desolation of that forsaking. It had all been just a youthful enthusiasm, an illusion, a madness. And now this was reality. If there was a God, he was not a God who cared. And into that emptiness there flooded all the darkness of the world and all its fear, and it overwhelmed Jesus. All the horrors of war and wickedness and slavery and child starvation, and the bitterness of cruelty and loneliness, and the horrors of captivity and condemnation, and all the sick hopelessness of sick humanity. All this – and the terrors and horrors of hell, which are beyond our imagining – all this came and swamped him, wholly and completely. All these things have their roots in sin, which is the rebellion against God's love, not only of you and me, but of Lucifer and his angels as well as all our forebears through all the world.

And then, from the depths of Jesus' need, there comes this extraordinary unreligious remark: 'I thirst.' This is the man who talked of living water – 'Whosoever drinketh of the water that I shall give him shall never thirst.' It was an awful fall from the glory of that triumphant certainty to that pleading cry. One of the soldiers dipped a sponge in the jar of rough wine standing there and Jesus drank. He had refused a drink before but the needs of the body can be utterly overwhelming, as most of us know.

Over the whole scene gradually came darkness and silence. The crowds had mostly gone away, so that the little group of Jesus' friends could come closer. And then, in the darkness and in the silence, all four gospels agree that suddenly there came a loud shout, a strong cry, a powerful voice, utterly unlike the quiet words that there had been before. And it was frightening, coming from that dying man upon the cross who had given up everything, who had had everything taken from him, who had cried for something to drink. This one word – 'Tetelestai', 'It is finished', 'It is consummated', 'It is completed', 'It is done'. However you translate it, it is a cry of triumph. He had done what he came to do: 'I must be about my Father's business.' It was finished, and complete, over and done with. And then he said, 'Father, into thy hands I commend my spirit.' The separation was not after all complete. The light broke in on him and he was able to say 'Father' again, not 'My God' but 'Father'. He had been all the way through. Every power on earth had been brought to bear on him, together with all the powers of hell and the darkness, to make him give up, but he would not. He completed what he had begun, and that is why we Christians have the cross as our sign. It is the sign of victory.

There are still too many people who think that on Good Friday death conquered, and all was sadness and blackness and darkness until the Good triumphed on Easter day. This is not true. The powers of evil, of pain, and of dereliction, failed to separate God from man there on the cross and Jesus died with a shout of triumph, commending himself to his father. Easter day is purely and simply the stamp of God's approval, the publication of victory.

That triumph is eternal but it needs to be renewed in our lives day by day. I can make a committal of myself to God on the day of my baptism or confirmation or ordination as a priest – on any day you like from Sunday to Saturday. But I have got to live out that committal for all the endless tomorrows. And I am so weak and so proud that I cannot fight the powers which tear and strain at love. I don't like giving myself and humbling myself and I am so independent that I don't want to be dependent and abandon myself to the power and love of God. So, by the end of even one day, my commitment is gone and my love is in shreds. Our love just is not the kind which can abandon itself wholly once and for all, whether it is for God or to a relationship like marriage.

I only wish it were, but we are not made like that. It's what being human means.

So the Christian has to offer the sacrifice of himself, in one with the sacrifice of Christ, every day of his life. 'I commit myself to you. What do you want of me?' 'You gave your body and blood. What can I give to you, Lord?' 'Do you want some of my fears? Some of my worries? Some of the securities to which I cling so tightly?' Because love soon grows cold. We need the fire of the Spirit, the tongues of flame to stir our hearts and make them burst into fire, and in the heart of the fire is the Christ and his triumphant affirmation of victory and love. Whether in a fiery furnace as Shadrach, Meshach and Abednego found him, walking free, or in an office or a factory or a traffic jam, Jesus is there. 'Lo, I am with you alway, even unto the end of the world.' In the last resort, the sacrifice is made and the barriers to love are overcome.

CHAPTER SIX

Holy mystery

We have talked a little about the nature of God and a little about the nature of man. We have also talked a little, and again not nearly enough, about the link which God himself has made with man in Jesus Christ, the Son of God and the Son of man, who in himself holds the two natures, human and divine, together. In him God has demonstrated the nature of his own being and the true nature of man by giving himself completely in order to break down the barrier between himself and the world. But Jesus knew that even in his lifetime his teaching fell on deaf ears – deaf not because people were unwilling to hear but because they had not learned to listen properly. His nature, his love, his complete self-giving, needed to be re-presented again and again to his own followers and to all the succeeding generations, in the simplest of simple actions, which not even the theologians can distort and confuse beyond a certain point, and through which we can very gradually learn to hear and see and experience the true nature of his love.

I believe it was for this reason that before he went out to betrayal and death Jesus initiated a mystery, an action, which he commanded his disciples to go on doing. We call it by any number of names and the name is not important. In this book I generally call it the Mass, because it is the word most associated with the idea of sacrifice, and this aspect of the Last Supper, as I explain below, seems to me to be more fundamental than any other.

I think it is important to emphasize that from its very beginning this last meal of Jesus with his disciples was a secret and mysterious thing. Jesus arranged it in such a way that no one knew in advance where it would take place. He told two of his disciples to follow a man carrying a pitcher of water to his home (a man doing women's work would have been an unusual sight and quite adequate as a recognition signal) and there they would find a room had been provided where they could make preparations for the meal. Clearly Jesus believed that this last meal was of vital importance in completing his life's work and so he made quite sure that Judas Iscariot was not able to betray him or his whereabouts to the authorities before he had finished what he had come to do.

When the meal was ready, Jesus led his disciples, including Judas, to that upper room and the first thing he did there was to take off his coat, tie a towel round his waist and wash his disciples' feet. Since the men were either barefoot or wearing sandals and had been walking through the excrement and filth of the streets, this was a revolting job and it was generally done by a slave who was too young or too old to be useful for anything else. At first Peter refused to let his Master wash his feet and was told in no uncertain terms that if he would not accept this service, he could not be one of Jesus' disciples.

When he had finished and had put his coat on again, Jesus said to them, 'Know ye what I have done to you? Ye call me Master and Lord: and ye say well; for so I am. If I then, your Lord and Master, have washed your feet; ye also ought to wash one another's feet.'

It has always seemed to me to be a great pity that, except on Maundy Thursday, the Church does not do anything in its liturgy to remind itself of this act and command of Jesus. Perhaps we would have kept a much clearer grasp on the essence of our faith through the centuries if we had recalled day by day that we can only live in the life of our Lord by giving and receiving from others the most humiliating service.

Later in the evening, after supper, Jesus took bread into his hands and said, 'This is my body which is given for you: this do in remembrance of me', and then he took the cup of wine and said, 'This is my blood of the new testament, which is shed for many for the remission of sins.' 'This do ye, as oft as ye drink it, in remembrance of me.'

Now a whole book could be written about those words, and indeed many books have been written about them. I only want to say two things here. First, notice that the words are 'This is my body which is given *for* you' and 'This is my blood . . . which is shed *for* many'. A lot of people are inclined to act as though they were 'This is my body which is given *to* you' and so lay the primary emphasis on receiving the consecrated elements in Holy Communion. Certainly Jesus told us to eat and drink these holy things, but the primary element is that his body and blood are given to death or to God *on behalf of* the disciples. He is doing this *for* them. So the main emphasis lies on the sacrificial aspect of his act.

Then there is this terribly important word *'anamnesis'*, which we translate as 'remembrance' simply because there is no other way of translating it. But it does not mean what we ordinarily mean by 'remembrance'. When we have a Remembrance Day we think back to the past and we remember with thankfulness the men who gave their lives for us in the Battle of Britain or something of that kind. To us, remembrance also has an element of nostalgia. We remember incidents from our childhood with affection or with regret. But the word that Jesus used when he said, 'This do in remembrance of me', has very little to do with the past. It means to 'recall'.

What Jesus is saying is 'Do this for the recalling of me, into the *present.*' This is his means, instituted by himself, which we can use at our volition to bring him, simply because he loves us, 'out of the everywhere into here', and into the 'now', into the lives which we are leading, into our situation, and indeed, when we receive him in Communion, into ourselves, for the feeding of our souls and bodies.

And of course when we are at the Communion rail we come into a new relationship, not only with God and those who are kneeling beside us, but with the whole of creation. We are brought into communion with him. There may not be many people geographically present but there are thousands throughout the world at any given moment making that same act of adoration; there are the angels and archangels and the whole company of heaven, together with the whole communion of saints, living and dead, and, in a wider circle still, every creature that God has ever made and ever will make. All he holds in his existence is in communion with us when we are in communion with him.

Each offering of the Mass at some particular place and time has therefore, I believe, eternal and cosmic significance. At the end of the last chapter I said that Christ's triumphant victory in breaking down the barriers between God and man is eternal. The new covenant of love was made once and for all on Calvary and does not need to be renewed, for God's love cannot fail. But the world's response fails constantly. It fails in each of us as individuals: 'By the end of even one day my commitment is gone and my love is in shreds.' And it fails in the whole body of mankind of which each of us is a part. It is we who need to renew our covenant relationship as children of God which we broke the day before.

The daily Mass is in one sense an act of renewing that covenant. Every day I 'do this in remembrance of him', and by doing so I claim from him all that he has promised in the covenant and I recall him into all that I am to do in the coming day. I do this not only for myself but also for those whom I love and those who live and work around me, for the rejects and failures and the inadequate, the proud and the rich and the happy, and for all who stand in need of the healing love of God, which is everyone. And I do most deeply believe, and have taught all through my ministry, that taking part in this daily renewal of the covenant is one of the greatest privileges which a Christian has and one of the most worthwhile offerings he can make.

This is *not* pious escapism, or at least it should not be. As I said at the end of the second chapter and cannot help going on saying all through this book, the tension between involvement with God and involvement with the world is the heart and core of the Christian life. The more agonizing or the more glorious the world's need and the world's beauty, the more we need to plunge ourselves into God – and the deeper our life in God, the greater our responsibility and joy in the world.

It seems to me that, whereas in the past the Church has over-emphasized its heavenward aspect, today many of us over-emphasize the earthward direction, and so the primary relationship with God, which is the source of all real community and life, is forgotten and we try to heave ourselves up by our own bootstrings. The revised liturgies, the 'parish communions', the 'family services', are all attempts to make us aware of our responsibility to be true Christians, true members of a community, brimming over with love and service. But all too often they flop because God has somehow got left out of it. The sense of the supernatural is missing in the life of the Church today. Perhaps I am just being blind and it really is there, underneath, but if so, it is very hard to find it in the modern liturgies, which seem to me to do very little to proclaim the mystery and glory of God. Their main object is, it seems, to be as short and simple as possible. Certainly I have no objection in principle to using words which are simple and straightforward and can be 'understood' by anyone (in so far as 'religious' words can be 'understood' at all). Nothing is more certain than that Jesus came for sinners, and among sinners are many simple men as well as many intellectuals. But if you take simplicity too far when dealing with the deepest mysteries of life you run into the danger of producing only a flat banality and I myself do not believe it is possible to proclaim the majesty and the love of God in a hurried and diluted form. Equally,

I do not think it is possible to enable someone, and especially a beginner in the faith, to feel that he has a 'real' part in what is being done simply by giving him more responses to make. How can he feel that he is 'adoring' – stretching out to something which is just beyond his reach, something to which he longs to reach forward – if it is put in front of him like a plate of porridge?

I, at any rate, find it almost impossible as a Christian priest to proclaim the mysteries of God to an inquirer and then to tell him with any confidence that he can begin to experience this mystery and have it set out before him at the eight o'clock service in his local parish church. He is, I'm afraid, likely to find a priest who arrives in the church five or ten minutes before the service starts, having apparently done nothing to prepare himself for his tremendous act of adoration and union, and a tiny handful of people, mostly old ladies, who represent the body of Christ on earth. Series Two (or whichever series it is by now) is briskly gone through in about twenty minutes, and in what often seems a machine-like way, and the priest then shakes our inquirer's hand, civilly asks if he is a visitor, and scarpers off to his breakfast without giving any apparent time to his own thanksgiving. This may be a caricature, but I don't think it is very much exaggerated, and it is not surprising that many people today (including, I suspect, many clergy) find it a totally meaningless exercise.

I am not sure that the supernatural would be very much more discernible if I sent my beginner to a 'parish communion'. He might well find a greater sense of community and fellowship and become aware that here is a human group, a company of people doing something together. But would the wonder, the awefulness of Christ's sacrifice and our recalling of it, our reaching up to God and his coming down to us, would this really get through? Would many parish priests really mind very much whether it was a family service or a parish communion, as long as people came to church and had a nice friendly get-together afterwards?

God forbid that I should despise nice friendly get-togethers, but they are not, as we so often try to pretend they are, the 'fellowship of the Holy Spirit'. The love of God which 'is shed abroad in our hearts' enables us to have a new kind of relationship with each other which is different from the old command, given to all men, that they should love their neighbours as themselves. This new relationship, which in the Greek is called *koinonia* and for which there is no adequate translation in English, is a total commitment. It is of the same order as the relationship between a man and his wife when they have truly become a part of each other. And when, through the flooding in of the Holy Spirit, this true fellowship has grown, love and service really do spill over in an irresistible flood into the world around, as has happened at Taizé or in the Focolare movement, or with some of the new Pentecostals, or with Mother Teresa and her sisters in Calcutta.

But this is a God-given love and it can only come if firstly, and most basically, we are turned towards him and not towards each other. So I myself think it is a pity that in our new liturgies we exchange the kiss of peace (which I love and value) before the consecration prayer and not after it. When the love of God has come among us we can offer each other *his* peace and go in that fellowship to the Communion rail. Without him we have nothing at all to give each other.

I feel the same regret about the placing of the Benedictus in the new liturgies – that great shout of welcome, 'Blessed is he that cometh in the name of the Lord. Hosanna in the highest!' In the old liturgies this was the great turning point of the Mass. Up to that point, from the confession of helplessness, 'Lord, have mercy', through listening to the word of God and professing faith in the Creed, and on through the offering of 'ourselves, our souls and bodies', the Church strove towards God, its worship

culminating in an act of adoration in which it joined
with the whole of redeemed creation: 'Holy, holy, holy,
Lord God of hosts, heaven and earth are full of thy
Glory: Glory be to thee, O Lord most high.' But that is
as far as any created being can go. There is no creature
on earth or in heaven that can ascend into the holy of
holies. And so in the old liturgies it was made clear that
God comes down to meet us, as he came in the Incarnation,
and so we welcomed him. 'Blessed is he that cometh in the
name of the Lord. Hosanna in the highest.' Then the words
of Christ's self-offering, the consecration of the bread and
wine, followed.

In the new liturgies this shout of welcome and praise
comes after the consecration, which seems to me to imply
that we can reach God under our own steam and, as it
were, make him become present in the consecrated
elements. Perhaps this arrangement does not matter too
much so long as we know what we are really doing and
are conscious that in the Mass we can find the heart of
adoration and join with Christ, our Master, Saviour,
Friend and Brother, in being lifted up to heights which we
by ourselves are quite incapable of reaching. But I do not
see how this is possible, how we can be aware that we
are in the centre of mystery, unless we have time to get
our eyes attuned to the darkness and our ears attuned
to the still, small voice of God, and are given words which
stretch out beyond our comprehension and lead us towards
adoration.

Perhaps if there was a great deal of silence in the service
a beginner would catch something of the holy mystery.
But at almost every celebration I have attended in recent
years there has been an almost perpetual noise of prayers
or responses or hymns, which seems almost designed to
prevent any true encounter between a seeker and the
Christ whom he seeks. Certainly, as far as the Anglican
Church is concerned, I would rather take that beginner
to a small house group celebrating the holy mysteries
round a kitchen table where I trusted the love of the few

people who might be gathered there and knew that they were a true community, or else to some glorious High Mass with a sense of mystery and wonder conveyed by music, incense, bells, and whatever other adjuncts may be helpful in lifting us out of the ordinary world, than send him to an ordinary Sunday morning service.

Certainly, I am not surprised that so many young people are being forced to go to new movements on the fringe of the Church or to go outside the institutional Church altogether when they are searching for a means of encountering the living Lord. Yet in one sense I believe it is impossible for any true seeker to go outside 'the Church', and I try to explain what I mean by this in the next chapter.

CHAPTER SEVEN

The company of the beloved

Once we begin to know that we are living in the love of God, we start belonging, whether we like it or not, to 'the Church'. For the Church in its widest sense is not this or that body of Christians who worship in a particular way. The Church is 'the communion of saints'. And if it gives you a shock to think of yourself as a potential saint, just remember that a saint is simply a sinner who knows that God loves him enough to have been crucified for him. So it is equally true to say that the Church is a 'communion of sinners', and I must admit that it is far more recognizable if we call it that.

There are of course many other names for the Church. It has been called 'the body of Christ', 'the new Israel', 'the household of God', and so forth, and all these names express different parts of the truth about it. I prefer 'the communion of saints' because it emphasizes two most important truths so clearly. The first is that all Christians are saints, which means that, however hypocritical or neurotic or just plain bad we may be, we know that we are loved and therefore redeemed and 'made holy' for the service of love. *But we cannot love by ourselves*. A saint by himself is a nonsense. Jesus told us that the distinguishing mark of his disciples is their love for each other and this is not the ordinary 'loving our neighbours as ourselves' which is required of all men, but 'the fellowship of the Holy Spirit', *Koinonia*, a belonging together at the depths of ourselves. So we have to be a *communion* of saints, bound together, belonging together, needing, trusting, accepting each other.

I do not believe that any of us, whether minister, priest or layman, can find God without also finding a 'company of the beloved' with whom he can in some way share his search. 'Where two or three are gathered together in my name,' said Jesus, '*there* am I in the midst.'

This is another paradox. I have already emphasized the utter necessity for every serious Christian to make time to be alone with God and I have expressed my own belief in the sacrifice of the Mass as the focal point of Christian life. But it is too easy to get bogged down in generalities and pious resolutions. We have to make actual the trust and forgiveness and love which we learn and express in private prayer and public worship by actually practising these things with our 'even Christians', as Julian of Norwich calls them.

This is the real test of love – to let others experience you as you really are and trust that they will accept you as God accepts you, and then in turn to seek truly to accept them as they are, dull, ugly, boring, stupid, and selfish though they may be, and, indeed, as you may be. The work of Jesus is to make men whole and the work of the Holy Spirit is to make men into a whole, to bring us closer and closer together until we find our unity with each other in him. These two kinds of healing go together and it just is not possible to be whole and isolated at the same time. Even the Greeks were aware of this, thousands of years ago. Their word for a private person, someone who is cut off from the rest, was '*idios*', from which we get the word 'idiot' – someone who is so mentally handicapped that he lives in a world of his own.

The idiocy of solitude is something which psychologists and psychiatrists are recognizing more and more. Treatment of neurosis and some kinds of mental illness is now seen to consist very largely of teaching people to find new ways of relationship. But many Christians are still unwilling to recognize that this is also true for them. They are prepared to turn to God to ask for forgiveness and healing, but they are not prepared to turn to their fellow-men. This is a question of pride. We will not humble ourselves sufficiently to ask healing from each other or open ourselves to each other so that healing can flow in.

Personally, I am sure that this kind of love and trust cannot be developed at real depth except in a small group. Jesus chose twelve men, and that I think is the maximum. Seven or eight is probably an easier number. It may be a prayer or study group which is an offshoot of a larger congregation. It may be three or four couples who live close together and who get together regularly, perhaps without any set belief, but who are trying to explore what meaning and purpose and love mean to them, and what they want them to mean to their children. It may be a group of people in the same job, perhaps using their lunch-hours to try and find out who they really are and why they are slogging away at whatever it is they are doing. It may be a group set up by some specific organization which exists to generate groups of this kind. I myself am the Warden of a non-denominational movement, the Servants of Christ the King, whose members are committed to learning to pray, talk and work together in this way.

I say more in the next chapter about how I think that membership of such a group strengthens a Christian's life and often is the only thing that makes it possible for him to keep going on. Here I am more concerned with the Church in a wider sense and I do believe that we are much more likely to make belonging and acceptance real in a larger congregation if we have already experienced it in a small group. Infection works for good as well as for bad, and if Christian love flourishes, and trust and healing begin to flow in a small group, they are bound to flow outwards to the wider congregation and to the wider world. Then the act of love which we make at the altar rail will have for each of us a kernel of experience of the cost of 'belonging' and 'relationship' and 'acceptance' about which we often talk so glibly.

I myself did not begin to realize the depth and width and gloriousness of the 'fellowship of the Spirit' until I found myself cut off from all natural human contact in the prison cells of the South African Security Police.

I stood each morning facing the two windows of my cell and I imagined a great crucifix hanging in front of me. And there I went through the words of the Mass. When the time came to do the actual things which Jesus taught us to do, in remembrance of him, I had no bread or wine to offer. But as I imagined myself taking these two common gifts I said the words which Jesus taught us to say: 'This is my body, this is my blood.' And the mysteries became alive.

The Communion which I received in that prison cell was real and magnifical in a way which I cannot begin to describe. As I said at the beginning of this book, I had a completely satisfying (or almost completely satisfying) knowledge that God *is*. But also, for the first time in my life, I began to realize what it means to worship 'with the whole company of heaven' in the Mass. I have always realized that it meant that we were in the company of the angels and the archangels and the other great glorious beings that are beyond our experience and also in the company of the great saints, and of Mary, the mother of Jesus, but I had never fully realized that the company of heaven included the company of the beloved here on earth. In so far as I had realized this, I had tended to visualize the company of heaven as members of the institutional Church and I had a fairly narrow view of what that meant. In that prison cell it became absolutely clear to me that the company of the beloved on earth, which is part of the company of heaven, consists of people of all sorts and kinds, every sort of Christian and possibly those who formally reject the Church but who are nevertheless numbered by Jesus amongst those whom he loves and saves.

I want to make it absolutely clear that to me these were real experiences and completely authentic. I also want to make it clear that they were both 'given' to me. I am neither a Bunyan nor a Bonhoeffer, as my book *Encoun-*

tering Darkness makes clear. The experience of the reality of the communion I received was given to me by God himself. The experience of the company of heaven, the company of the beloved, cannot, it seems to me, have been anything other than the prayers of thousands of people, which were being said for me in churches all over the world, coming through the concrete walls of my cell and filling the place with love so that, although I was in solitary confinement, I have never had such a sense of 'belonging' in all my life.

I tried to put some of the wonder of all of this into my prison diary:

> I've never understood this business of being 'conscious' that other people are praying for one – but I am very constantly conscious of it here – not so much at periods of stress, e.g. in questioning when my mind just goes blank (mostly I think with fear . . .) but when I'm alone and particularly at night and I suppose at 'Mass' . . . Somehow the great words like Love and Peace take on an unduly different dimension. It's not that I feel Love or Peace in any way really : but it's as 'attributes' of God they seem much more real – more intrinsic to him . . . I do feel very much loved by some – at this moment a lot – of people . . . Perhaps I am wrong but I had the feeling this morning that there were thousands of Christians throughout the world with me – a most extraordinary, glorious, truly comforting and strengthening feeling – although I know I must not be dependent upon feelings (*Encountering Darkness*, pp. 264-9).

This new experience of the meaning of *koinonia* was reinforced for me after I was released from prison and was awaiting trial. As I have tried to describe in my autobiography, love and prayer flooded in from people of every denomination and from all over the world, while in Johannesburg itself Christians, who ranged from Roman Catholics to Quakers and back again, came together not only to worship but to protest, to think and to work together for the Church and State in the Republic of South Africa.

For this reason, I am not concerned, as perhaps I ought to be, with schemes for unity. It seems to me that the Church's divisions originate in the mistake of coming down too hard and exclusively in favour of one particular aspect of a paradoxical truth and then refusing to admit the validity of the other aspects. Some stress the need for morality and self-discipline, and others the helplessness or sinfulness of man; some stress the sacrificial aspect of the Mass and others emphasize Communion. There are differences not only of theology but also of temperament. Some, like myself, are insecure and need hierarchy and order in their Church organization and others feel stifled by it. Some have hearts which are lifted up by the music and ceremonial of a solemn Mass and others prefer to worship God in the glorious silence of a Quaker meeting. The important thing is that, whether or not we use the outward and visible signs of the sacraments, we do lay hold of the sacrifice which Jesus made for us upon the cross and that we do it by the means which has most meaning and reality for us. I have no doubt whatsoever that if our worship is the best which we are capable of offering and if we who offer it accept each other in love, the Lord God accepts us.

None of the differences in temperament or theological emphasis need divide us were it not for sin, which, as I have said, always divides and always separates. And the barriers created by sin can only be broken down by sacrificial love. I do not believe that they can be over-come by plans and schemes and written agreements. In fact, I am much inclined to agree with those who say that the Church will become one only when it has become so loving that the world rejects it. It has been shown all over the world that where and when the Church is persecuted, it finds that its divisions are meaningless in the face of its concern for God and its attempt to love God and God's creation.

This brings us slap up against the tremendous paradoxicality of the Church. The Church *is* the body of Christ, the means by which the love of God is made actual in the world. It is meant to be a point of infection – the focus of reconciliation and renewal and hope for all the torn, aching and suffering world. It exists to proclaim, exercise and administer the love of God and the glorious liberty of his children. But its members are, by definition, sinners, and the effect of their combined sinfulness is only too clear. Instead of digging well-springs of liberty and love, we have made ourselves prisons (we literally think of churches as stone buildings) in which we Christians wall ourselves up to shut out everything about the modern world which threatens our security. So many of us are afraid to move, to take in new ideas or to test old ones. Often we are afraid even to talk about our religion because in our hearts we are not at all sure that it will stand examination by modern ways of thinking. We do not trust God enough to be willing to move, and love must involve movement if the lover and the beloved are to come together. Sloth, fear and a divided heart are deadly sins for the whole Church as well as for individual Christians.

So it happens that all too often the Church is one of the great obstacles to the Christian faith in the mind of modern man. People, especially young people, who have 'found' Jesus as a living being, or who are seeking for some meaning to their lives, look at the Church and ask what it has to do with this living being whom they have found? And so they go off to join one of the Christian communes, or the 'Jesus people', or try to find a living faith in one of the oriental religions which in the West have not yet got bogged down in an institutional swamp. I am sure that this is what I would have done myself if I had been born forty years later and had found the meaning of life in Jesus in the 1970s instead of the 1930s. But I am truly and deeply thankful that as no alternatives existed in the 1930s, I found my way through Jesus back into the institutional Church, and gradually learnt to love it and to believe that it is an essential part of the Christian religion and part of the dispensation of God for man.

I believe this because of the amount of time which Jesus spent with his beloved twelve in and around the holy land, time which he could have used proclaiming his gospel throughout the then civilized world, and I believe it because of his declaration that he was going to build his Church upon a rock and that 'the gates of hell shall not prevail against it'. This has proved true. Hell has challenged the Church's strength over and over again. Men and women have suffered and died for their faith, from the early Christian martyrs to those in the Soviet Union or South Africa or Greece or Brazil or Uganda who are being tortured and imprisoned and executed for their faith today. But much more dangerous than this to the Church's life has been the corruption from within – its own burning and torturing, and its own hatred and petrification and self-idolatry. *And yet* the Church still lives. Still converts are made and the gospel of love and forgiveness is proclaimed and the Mass is celebrated and the truth is handed on. It is not the pale Galilean of two thousand years ago but the living, ascended, risen, glorious Jesus who pours himself into the Church, and the Church strives and struggles to receive him and reflect him to the world. It is a living interchange between two living beings.

So although the Church is the body of Christ in the world, Christ and the Church are not interchangeable terms. It is the Church's job to witness to Jesus, to present him to the world in words, to make him present in the sacraments and to demonstrate his love to all creation. But Jesus is not confined to his Church. He also stands over against it in permanent challenge, criticism and love. He is the way and the truth, and the world rightly will not let us forget this fact. 'What has *this* got to do with Jesus?' is the question which those of us who call ourselves churchmen need to ask ourselves every day of our lives.

But it is not good enough just to ask the question, we also have to do something about it. One of the reasons why I myself felt that I had to be a priest was that I was convinced it was not good enough to stand outside the Church criticizing it. I could see the Church appearing to live happily with the contradiction between life in Johannesburg, the city of gold, and the Christian life, and I felt that I had to get right into the Church, into its very heart if possible, and try to put it right from there. That I have failed to do so is obvious, but I am still trying and so are millions of members of the communion of saintly sinners (or sinning saints) throughout the world.

Clergymen are always telling their congregation that it's no good blaming them for the faults of the Church or the deadness of some denominational group of Christians, because the responsibility lies on the whole people of God, ordained or not. This is certainly true, and I have often said myself in South Africa when people asked, 'Why doesn't the Church do something?' – meaning, 'Why don't the clergy make a stand?' – that it just is not possible for a priest or minister to go very much further or faster than his congregation are willing to go with him.

Nevertheless, I am sure that it is part of the particular responsibility of priests and ministers, as the trained, paid servants of the Church, to hold the tension between earth-centredness and heaven-centredness – to walk confidently and surely in both the natural and supernatural worlds. Just as a doctor has six years' training to enable him to understand the basic functioning of the body, so we clergy are supposed to understand the functioning of the whole man – not as specialists but as practical advisers who know the natural and supernatural ropes. We need ourselves to be men who at least try to walk with God and pray and talk with him (and who are *seen* to be so), but we should also be capable of helping others to go about these things. We may not have mystical gifts ourselves but we ought to be able to discern those who have, and pass them on to specialists if they need deeper instruction in the Way than we are capable of giving. But equally, we should be able to talk with men where they really are, with their real needs and fears.

What we clergy need now, more than anything else, is courage: The courage to proclaim the vision which we had when we entered the priesthood. And where, in earthly terms, are we to get it from? The bishops and the theological colleges could certainly do more to encourage us – if they were not so frightened themselves – but most of all, we need the courage of the laity. We need people who are honest enough with themselves and us to say, 'Look, we don't need you to teach us how to run tenants' associations or organize charity collections. We can probably do it better than you can anyway. We do need to think about the purpose of our existence, in the face of our boredom and loneliness and fear, and also in the face of our joy and strength and confidence. We need to find our real selves, and *you're* supposed to be able to help us.'

Many of us, and certainly myself, would not find such a challenge easy to cope with. We know in our hearts how far we are from finding any real answers, even for ourselves and in our own lives, and how blindly and half-heartedly we reach out to the mystery at the heart of being. And we are often afraid to say so. Instead of trusting our congregations with our own blindness and weakness, we trot out neat 'logical' explanations of the inexplicable and then complain because people are bored and dissatisfied with them. But the Christian faith, as I have tried to say over and over again in this book, is not a series of neatly packaged 'truths' to be swallowed whole. It is a search which, except for the greatest mystics, it is impossible to prosecute alone.

One thing I am sure about. If we Christians really believed in the love and forgiveness of God which we proclaim so glibly, our churches would be much odder, madder and more joyful places than they are now.

When I was talking about the Lord the Spirit, I referred to the first impression that the Church made on the pagan and Jewish world. It was not that these Christians were wise or good or holy or respectable, but that they were drunk! Drunk! At that hour in the morning! And Peter had to explain that they weren't – though they might be behaving as if they were. That was the first effect of the Church. The same thing happened with St Francis and his friars. No one thought of them as holy at first. 'You're mad', they said, '– living the way you do.' And they said the same thing of Jesus himself. 'He is beside himself – he's schizophrenic.' St Paul told the Ephesians, 'Be not drunk with wine . . . but be filled with the Spirit', presumably implying that the outward effect was much the same, and St Ignatius Loyola says in his lovely prayer, the *Anima Christi*, 'Soul of Christ, sanctify me; body of Christ, save me; *blood of Christ, inebriate me.*'

I believe that this element of reckless joy has not only been neglected by the institutional Church but has been deliberately suppressed (the Pentecostalists who have begun to recapture it are certainly looked on with a good deal of suspicion). We want to confine the Lord the Spirit – tie him down and tidy him up so that he only blows where and when it is safe and convenient and proper and not likely to cause comment or offence. But the Spirit bloweth where he listeth, and if the Churches do not want him he will blow on the 'Jesus people' and the hippie communes and the mental hospitals and the prisons, and leave the Churches to their respectability, too solid and rigid and heavy to move.

The ability to move is, I believe, the concomitant of love, and therefore *the* essential necessity for the Church. Throughout the last two thousand years, great men like St Francis and John Wesley and many others have given us a great heave, and each time, because we are sinners as well as saints, we have shrugged off the pressures which were trying to shake us out of our torpor and have relapsed back into cosy immobility. We are so careful. We conserve our beliefs, our money, our future, our membership; we do anything to avoid 'rocking the boat'. It is a conscientious conservation. We honestly care that the beliefs and institutions which we value should survive, but we do not trust the promise of Jesus that, *whatever happens*, the gates of hell shall not prevail against the Church. If we really believed this, we would be more able to leave the Lord Jesus to protect his own, we would look for holiness rather than scholarship or administrative ability amongst our leaders (necessary as these two things are), and above all we would concentrate not on maintaining the fabric of our institutions but on preaching God's good news of deliverance, the glorious liberty of the children of God.

Of course, there is another side – as there always is in any human business. We need something solid which makes demands on our minds and hearts and wills. (Certainly, this is one of the reasons why I myself came back to the Church rather than remaining content with the 'wideness' of Toc H.) Many of the youngsters are coming back because they are fed up with the permissive society and the 'new' morality. They want something spelt out. But rules are only secondary – even the ten commandments and the law of love which Jesus himself taught us. They make no sense unless the reckless joy of self-giving, forgiveness, love, acceptance, *koinonia*, are primary and are seen to be primary in the life and teaching of the Church.

CHAPTER EIGHT

Choice

The difficulty with becoming a Christian, as with so many other things, is knowing just how and where to begin. I suggested earlier in this book that one very good way to start is by making an attempt to pray, but you, if you want to start at all, may choose to start in some other way. The important word, of course, is 'choose'. We all have a tendency, particularly nowadays, to excuse ourselves by saying, 'It wasn't my fault – I'm made like that – I really can't help it.' 'It's all the fault of my brains or my health or upbringing or education or environment.' And so we deny that we have any real power of choice.

Of course there is a great deal of truth in all this, as God knows far more clearly than we can know ourselves. We are a mixture and we were made that way, as I tried to explain when I was talking about the human paradox in the first chapter of this book. There is, if you like to think of it in that way, an 'I' and 'me' inside each of us. The 'I' is made in the image of God, the true person, the potential lover, the beloved. And the 'me' is what 'I' have become – the one who always wants to go after the immediate pleasure, the short-term end, the thing which 'I' don't really enjoy doing but still do almost in spite of myself. Some parts of the 'me' we have some control over if we really want to, and some we have very little control over at all – they may be the result of genetic inheritance or being 'spoilt' in some way in childhood; we may not even know that they are there until some sudden act or desire horrifies us. And of course the 'me' is affected by the experience and choices of every day –

ingrained habits and surroundings which make it hard to start behaving any differently, and which make change, *metanoia*, turning round, very hard indeed.

Perhaps the part of ourselves which is most paradoxical and in which it is hardest to keep the 'me' from swamping the 'I' is our sexual nature. Sex is of course an immensely strong drive and a fierce and demanding pleasure – as it has to be in order to ensure that the human race or any other species survives at all. And therefore, of all the parts of the psyche, it is the hardest to direct outwards in love and liberation and joy rather than inwards as a lust, a self-indulgence which is cut off from all real relationship and commitment so that both partners are simply used as 'things', and both become more subhuman as a result.

Christians should rejoice in their sexuality as a God-given means of expressing love, whether it is used as the ultimate expression of commitment between two people in sexual intercourse or as a source of creative energy or as a well of adoration. The great contemplatives were men and women who used their sexual energy as a vehicle for their love of God. They did not decry it or run away from it. They rejoiced in it and did so gloriously. You have only to read the Song of Solomon in the Bible or the writings of some of the great mystics, such as Raymond Lull's *Book of the Lover and the Beloved*, to see how true this is.

Unlike the animals, we human beings do have a choice in the use which we make of our sexual drives. (In some 'seductive' situations the urge may be so overwhelming that we do not feel we have a real choice, but we *can* avoid getting into such situations if we want to.) However, it is true that some people do have sexual natures which are extraordinarily difficult to cope with, and this is particularly true for men and women who are homosexual. Homosexuality is not wrong in itself and people are born or become homosexual through no fault of their own. They often have a very great capacity for love and by the same token a very great capacity for hate and jealousy, and it is extremely difficult for them to know how to use their love and sexuality so that it creates instead of destroying. Some people come to terms with this quite gloriously. I think particularly of two women whom I knew who lived together all their lives. I watched one of them dying of cancer while her friend nursed her, and I have never seen a greater example of lovingkindness in practice than they showed.

Basically, the choice is whether we use our sexuality to create or destroy; it is as simple, though alas not so easy, as that, for the pulls downwards of the 'me' can be quite terrifyingly strong, as I know only too well myself. In my own opinion, the worst damage is done not by casual relationships between single people, or even the use of women for prostitution, but by adultery where one of the partners still has an ongoing marriage. In the ten commandments adultery comes between murder and theft and it is very well placed. Adultery is a form of both stealing and killing since it takes and uses a man or woman who is already committed to somebody else and begins to destroy the 'one person' that his or her marriage has made and the family of which he or she is a part.

I don't want to go on and on about sex, important though it is, because it is only one aspect of our natures and its importance in relation to sin can be greatly exaggerated. As I tried to say earlier, sloth and refusal to change and double-mindedness can be much more deadly sins because they are much more obvious and we can continue to feel 'moral' when we commit them and bask in a glow of self-righteousness which adulterers at least are free from.

None of us is righteous. That is one of the basic teachings of the gospel and it is one of the great well-springs of Christian joy and liberation. Jesus showed us that God is loving and that he accepts and loves us as we are, *not* on condition that we are well-behaved. The choice which we have to make (and go on making all through our lives) is not whether or not to be 'good', but whether we will

accept or reject this love; whether we are going to explore, test, experiment, open ourselves to the experience
of being loved, learn to trust and reach out to love – rather
as an adopted child might learn to love and trust in his
new home, or stay closed up, slamming the door on all
that kid's stuff. 'I'm all right, I don't need anyone.' 'I'm
not going to risk being let down' – and so we condemn
ourselves to isolation. Of course, most people avoid
choosing the way of death quite as deliberately as that.
They simply avoid encountering love and follow the easy
undemanding crowd, doing what everyone else does and
all the time getting sucked further and further down until
change really does become almost impossible.

Not all the difficulties in the way come from inside
ourselves. Friends and families and people we work with
can make it desperately hard to keep going on. I remember
very clearly when I first became a Christian how much
it hurt when one of the typists in the office where I worked
told me that I wasn't nearly so much fun since I had got
bitten by religion. And I suppose in a sense she was right.
I did have a much deeper sense of joy than I had ever
experienced before but I could not be nearly as easy-going
about what went on in the office as I had been as a pagan.

I have often thought that the story of the three wise
men who followed the star to Bethlehem is a very good
parable of the problems which arise when one begins to
take Christ seriously. To start with, their wives must have
complained bitterly about their going off on a wild-goose
chase after a star, when it was obviously their duty to
stay at home with their families and the people around
who needed them. When they did get away and reached
what they thought was their destination, Jerusalem, the
holy city, they found the people there extremely snooty
and unwelcoming, as many well-established congregations
are when they are faced with newcomers who ask awkward questions and challenge long-held ideas. And finally,
when the wise men did at last get to Bethlehem, what they
found there was not the great glory they had expected

but a small baby in a smelly stable. 'How *can* this be the King of kings and Lord of lords?' must have been as much a question in their minds as it is in ours when we look round the Sunday congregation of a parish church and ask ourselves, 'How can the Lord God Almighty be *here*?'

But whatever their doubts and disappointments, the wise men did the best possible thing they could have done. 'When they were come into the house, they saw the young child with Mary his mother, and fell down, and worshipped him: and when they had opened their treasures, they presented unto him gifts: gold, and frankincense and myrrh.' That is the only thing to do when the bottom has dropped out of your faith. Force yourself to go flat on your face (metaphorically if not literally) in worship and offer *everything*. Gold, which symbolizes all material things, money, jobs, talents, possessions, and so on; incense, which represents all the lovely things, the love and friendship and beauty, hopes and desires, and the glorious golden memories of times when we felt most real and did know for certain that God is real and loving and the world is lovely. And then we offer the myrrh, which perhaps at such times is what we mostly have. Myrrh is a resin used for anointing the dead and to me it represents our sorrows and sins, our lusts and fears, pain and futility, and all our boredom and frustration. If you can force yourself to offer these three parts of yourself, regardless of whether you feel there is anyone to offer them to, you will find that your gift is accepted and that you have at least the strength to go on in hope 'to your own country'.

Another important thing to remember is that there were three wise men, not one. The tradition says that they came from different parts of the East and that one of them was black-skinned. They did not choose each other, they did not necessarily even like each other, but they came together because they were all going in the same direction and they *needed* each other. As I have said again and again in this book, it is virtually impossible to be a Christian by oneself. We are meant to belong to each other and to experience God's forgiveness and love and acceptance through learning to forgive and love and accept each other. Being part of a Christian group is sometimes the only way of hanging on to faith when depression or sin, or perhaps the strain of letting go old ways of thinking and finding more real and adult ones, gets too much for us.

Do you remember the story of 'doubting Thomas' – the apostle who was not with the others when Jesus came to them after the resurrection? Evidently he had 'had it' – in chunks. He was fed up with Jesus for getting himself crucified, fed up with the whole miserable business and perhaps most of all fed up with himself. He wanted nothing more to do with the other disciples and he just didn't want to know when they came and told him, 'We have seen the Lord.' But they almost literally dragged him back into their group, so that when Jesus came again, Thomas could not help encountering him and acknowledging him 'my Lord and my God'. But if it had not been for the others, Thomas would have gone drearily back to Galilee and never have known the risen Christ. Although they had to come in search of him, he had to love and trust them enough to go back with them. We cannot carry on without the sort of fellowship which I described in the last chapter. The problem is to find it, use it and stick with it.

Of course, the obvious place to look for 'the company of the beloved' is in a church congregation but one of the difficulties about this is that it is also 'the company of sinners'. It is sinners whom Jesus came to call, and it does often seem that the most peculiar people respond. So in whatever church we choose to explore we will find lots of people who are odd or nasty or difficult or awkward or just plain boring. And what else can we expect? After all, they probably don't like us much either. But two things remain true. One is that the better we get to know people, really to know them and allow them to know us, the more it becomes possible to begin to love them, even if we still don't much like them. And the other is that, like the three wise men, we are stuck with each other. True, we can wander from group to group and congregation to congregation looking for perfect soul-mates, and there may be a good case for looking around a bit before we settle down (as there is before marriage!), but if we are looking for perfect saints we won't find them.

Many people who have read this far are likely to be saying to themselves, 'Yes, this is all very well – all this about adoration and responding and growing in love and belonging, and so forth – but you just don't know *me*. I'm not that sort of person. I can't even do slimming exercises or stick to a diet for more than a couple of days', or 'I really can't *stand* people who bore me', or 'I have never really loved anyone in my life and I certainly can't see myself loving anything as nebulous as this God you keep talking about', or some other rather longing but hopeless reaction of this kind.

It is a good reaction, because it is at least realistic and Jesus did tell us to sit down and count the cost before we chase off in search of the kingdom of heaven. But there are several things to be said about it.

To start with, there are in my view two aspects to Christian commitment, two different ways of moving along the road of love – we might call them the long jump and the wriggle – and we have to be able to use both. The jump is when some major decision of self-offering and self-commitment has to be made: 'I am going to start behaving as if a loving God exists', or 'I am going to let go some relationship or ambition which I know will destroy me if I hang on to it', or 'I am going to face this terrible sorrow or illness which has come to me instead of hiding from it.' 'Let us go to him, oh my soul, with giant strides', says St Philip Neri, and there are times in our lives when there is no way of going slow. We have to make a giant stride or stay stuck in the mud. But after each stride there is always a period of wriggling, creeping along on our bellies, inch by painful inch, and sometimes feeling as if we are going backwards. Having made what felt like a great jump, we find that all our habitual sins and sloths catch up on us and try to drag us back, and although we do try to avoid them, we don't really try very hard, so that we go on committing them again and again and again.

Here there are two vital things to be done. The first is not to give up altogether – that is the only real failure. As long as you are still on the road and facing in the right direction, even if you feel as if you are slipping backwards, that is what really matters. Giving up *is* defeat, trying and failing is not. You may die with your sins totally unconquered, but so what? We are redeemed by the love of God, not by our own virtues, and if we are truly trying to open ourselves to that love, that is the only thing that matters.

Secondly, it is important to be definite and realistic about change. Of course God wants the whole of us – all the parts which we grab and clutch and try to hang on to – and so we do have to remember, as we turn to Christ in commitment, and as we pray and worship, that we are called to offer our whole selves. But we do have a lot in common with St Augustine, who prayed, 'Oh God, make me good, but not yet', and it is equally important to remember that we are not going to become holy overnight. If we try to abandon all our habits and selfishness in one fell swoop, we shall just find it impossible and give up. So we have to wriggle our way along.

It is much more effective to say, 'I know I come back from work exhausted and grumpy every evening. But from now on I will at least really look at my wife when I come in, and give her a proper kiss and say one nice thing to somebody before I start complaining that the tea isn't ready or cursing the children for making a racket.' Or, 'I can't stand my mother-in-law and I probably never will learn to love her, but I can invite her to tea every other week and keep my temper with her for two and a half hours by the clock.' And these wriggles are the beginning of real change because they are solid. One can look back at the end of the day and think whether one has done them or not, and if not, why not. (It is also surprising what a difference they can make to a relationship. People do respond to love even when it is given with an effort of the will, and what began as a chore can become a pleasure and even a joy.)

It is very important to take things day by day. Alcoholics are taught to say, *not* 'I will *never* have a drink again', but 'I will not have a drink *today*' – and we are all alcoholics as far as sin is concerned. The important thing is to start each day by renewing the covenant of love, offering ourselves, our souls and bodies to be made one with Christ's offering to our Father. That is all we can do, for there is no such thing as a 'do-it-yourself' Christian. Day after day, of course, we snatch back that offering almost as soon as it is made, but if we honestly *try* to mean it, the transforming power of the Lord the Spirit does gradually, imperceptibly, begin to take over.

Part of our wriggling will, of course, be trying to have enough self-discipline to make such an act of self-committal every day and to set aside a definite time for prayer and reading. I believe that this is absolutely essential for anyone who wants to encounter love, just as having a regular time for study and practice is essential for anyone who wants to be a musician or artist or acquire any other kind of skill. Keeping this time may be one of the greatest struggles that we have. It will certainly be something that the Devil will try his very hardest to prevent us from doing. Because once we are really trying to pray, day by day, and sticking to it, the Devil has had it, and he knows it.

I myself believe that it is equally essential to become a full member of some part of the Christian Church and to have a clear rule about attending its worship and receiving the Holy Communion regularly, with a proper period of preparation beforehand and a real act of realization and 're-collection' afterwards – but then I am, both by profession and temperament, a 'churchman', and it may take quite a long time of personal prayer and growth before a new Christian comes to feel the need for this, if he does at all.

There is another sacrament (a sacrament is an 'outward and visible sign of an inward and spiritual grace') that I myself have found to be of enormous help in enabling me to keep on keeping on, though making use of it for the first time is likely to feel much more of a giant stride than a wriggle – at least it did to me. And this is the sacrament of penance – the act of confessing one's sins and failures before a priest and receiving from him the assurance of God's forgiveness.

I fought with myself for several years before I made my first confession. I hated the thought of someone else knowing what I was really like inside and the shame of having to tell him, and I kept telling myself how the sacrament had been abused in the past and that if I honestly confessed my sins privately by myself, that was enough. But somehow I could not let it go at that. It was all very well saying that I could show I was sorry for my sins by ceasing to commit them, but I found I perpetually went on sinning, as I do today, and the only thing I could do to show that I really did care about it was to make my confession. So I finally summoned up my courage, prepared what I needed to say about my past life, and went and said it before a priest. It was a pretty traumatic experience but I think I can truly say that it was one of the greatest steps that I took in my religious life.

For some people, the thought of doing this will be so repugnant to their temperament and upbringing that it will seem quite impossible, and certainly the Anglican Church teaches that it is not *necessary*. It is a means of grace to be used by those who need it. But I have found that if people do make their confessions when they are confirmed, or when they return as adults to practising Christianity, or when they have come to a new awareness of what their faith means, the fact that they have made a really costing act of repentance and humility does make their commitment to Christ much more real and lasting. It is also a great help to obsessional characters that they don't have to agonize over whether they really *feel* sorry for their sins, because at least they are doing something to show that they *are* sorry. And the fact of having to think what to say and then say it does mean that the penitent really has to look at himself, his whole self, clearly in the light of love. Confession is a very concrete, unsentimental business and those who practise it find out a lot about themselves (good as well as bad) in the act of preparing and making it.

Perhaps even more important than this is that in the act of trusting a priest, a fellow human being, and finding that he has been through the same sort of thing himself and does understand, a penitent experiences *koinonia*, 'the fellowship of the Holy Spirit', on a very deep level. You *know* that you are accepted and beloved whatever you may have done. There is a wonderful sense of lightness and freedom after receiving absolution – of knowing that you are free to make a fresh start and that the power of God will be with you to help you do at least a little better than before.

I have talked a good deal in this book, and particularly in this chapter, about the way in which turning towards love inevitably involves change and about how we can begin to deal with the resistance to change which we call sin. But there are other difficulties in practising the Christian faith which are not in themselves sins, and in particular there are doubts and fears.

Everyone has doubts, including the clergy. We would not be human if we did not, and certainly without them we would not learn to stretch and grow in our faith and to hold on through the bad patches. 'Is it really true? How can all these paradoxical contradictions be held together?' and so on. I think it is often best in the first instance to ignore thoughts like this as passing jabs from the Devil and simply focus your thinking and prayer on what you do know to be true until whatever has been worrying you falls into place. But if this does not work and the doubt is really bothering you and hindering your prayer, then you should face it. Work out in your own mind just exactly what it is that you are troubled about. ('Doubts' in the vague, woolly abstract are simply one more attempt by the 'me' part of the personality to get the 'I' off its back.) And when you have sorted out the problem, get down to some serious study about it. You will find that people have written books about it or that some saint has worked it through in his own life, and that none of your ideas and worries are nearly as new or as shattering as you thought they were.

Many doubts spring from the impossibility of reconciling two sides of a paradox, and the most common example of this is the question, 'How can I believe God is good and all-powerful when I can see that the world is so full of evil and suffering?' We have all got to come to terms with this particular problem and many great books have been written about it. The one I know best is Austen Farrer's *Love Almighty and Ills Unlimited*, and if you are seriously bothered by this question, I would advise you to read it.

My own personal way of looking at the problem is derived from a number of sources and though it means something to me, it may mean nothing whatsoever to you. I know that 'God so loved the world, that he gave his only begotten Son . . .' – that he endured in his own flesh the deepest suffering that man can bear. And I know, as I said when I was talking about intercessory prayer, that God cannot desire his children to suffer. Tragedy is never God's will and if we look closely at the evil and suffering in the world we see that a great deal of it is the consequence of man's self-will. A great deal of illness is caused by factors in our own psyche or by the way we live our lives or the environment we have to live in. And much suffering is caused by greed or ignorance or sheer carelessness in the way in which man treats man or treats the planet and its resources. Also, as I said in the first chapter of this book, I believe that there are great powers of evil abroad in creation which are in bitter conflict with the healing forces of love.

None of this really satisfies the nagging question of apparently useless and uncaused pain. The earthquake which shatters a city, the child born with a broken body, the long-drawn-out illnesses which seem to destroy a personality before our eyes and leave a vegetable instead of the person we had loved, the utter agony of mental illness in someone we love. I do not believe that there are any easy, slick, logical answers, and perhaps in the end all we can do is to try and make bearing the pain an act of love while at the same time we complain furiously to God about our anger and hurt and inability to understand *why*. But most of us do have to try and understand because that is the way we are made, and personally I find that it helps to be aware that there is a reality in the phrase 'the body of mankind'. Although each one of us is a separate individual and is loved and known as a person, we are also a part of a whole, inextricably bound up, whether we like it or not, with every other human being in the world and indeed with the whole of creation. I know that if there is some infection in my own body it is a very good thing, even though it may be extremely painful, if the infection is drawn together into an abscess or boil, because the poison is being drained into one place where it can be dealt with and my body as a result is healed. And I believe that those who suffer apparently uselessly and needlessly are in some way absorbing and drawing out evil from the body of mankind.

To me, this makes some sense of the suffering of the helpless and particularly of children. If an evil man suffers he will rebel violently against his fate and, as it were, push the evil back into the system with an increment of his own bitterness and resentment. A Christian who endures his own pain or bears and cares for the pain of others can struggle, as Jesus struggled, to offer the prayer of Gethsemane, 'My Father, if this cup may not pass away from me, except I drink it, thy will be done' – and the sacrifice which began with that prayer redeemed the world. But children, and people who are helpless in mind, have not got the conscious ability either to rebel or to accept their pain; they just absorb and go on absorbing the poison of the world. And of course, if one only believes in this life, that is just sheer tragedy. But Christians believe that this life is only the beginning, though a very real part, of eternal life, and who can guess at the glory which is to come for those whose endurance has helped to heal the world? I have always disliked the saying 'Blessed are the meek' because meekness sounds so wishy-washy. But if one thinks of the meek as those who can suffer without rebellion, then they are indeed blessed because they are achieving more for the world than the courage, wisdom and sanctity of the greatest preacher or social reformer.

However hard we struggle to understand, doubts will always be with us, and the same is true of fear. It is *not* unchristian to be afraid – we know that Jesus himself was and so we need not be ashamed of it ourselves. Some people are much more troubled by fears than others and it seems to be largely a matter of temperament and emotional security rather than faith or will-power. I really do know what I am talking about on this subject because I have been told that I am an obsessional neurotic and I have been plagued all my life both by overwhelming panics and by nagging anxieties that everything I am responsible for is certain to go wrong. I am the sort of person who arrives at a railway station an hour before the train leaves and worries about a sermon I am supposed to be preaching next year.

But I have discovered that there are two levels of fear. The superficial kind, whether it is neurotic or a response to real danger of some kind, and a much deeper, more basic level where we can't bear to face ourselves or life or God and shut ourselves up in a tight little cage where we hope we can't be got at and be hurt. The superficial kind can be helped by psychotherapy, if it is a really crippling neurosis, or by taking our fear in our hands and facing the danger as if it were a real threat of some kind. But if it is not really serious, the best thing to do is often to accept it and live with it. There is a very good little paperback by a psychiatrist whose name I have forgotten, called *Be Glad You're Neurotic*, and this is good advice. At least being neurotic probably means that you do catch your trains and get your work done on time or leave the house securely locked with the gas taps turned off, or whatever it may be that you get bothered about. The real harm comes when you get an anxiety neurosis about having an anxiety neurosis! Then you are really in the soup.

It is with this acceptance of yourself as you are, neurosis and all, as well as with the deep underlying fears about death and old age and bereavement and the pain which comes from trying to grow in love, that the Christian faith helps. Peace is one of the great words of the New Testament. It was the song the angels sang at the Christ's birth, and on the last night of his life Jesus said to his disciples, 'Peace I leave with you, my peace I give unto you . . . Let not your heart be troubled, neither let it be afraid.' But, as with many other great words, 'peace' has become devalued. The word Jesus used was 'shalom', not a weak, vague neutrality, a cessation of hostilities, but a Messianic peace, the rule of the victor who has broken the chains of death and hell and shattered their power. 'Perfect love casteth out fear: because fear hath torment.' And so we have to sink our frightened, shivering selves in the strength and power of God: to repeat over and over again, until it has sunk deep into our consciousness, some phrase which assures us that 'underneath are the everlasting arms' and that we will not be allowed to fall or to be tested beyond our strength to bear it. Above all, we have to hang on to Jesus, as a frightened child hangs on to its mother, and know that as long as we can keep

with him we shall be all right. But that, like everything
else in the Christian life, does mean committing the whole
of ourselves. A frightened child does not cling with one
finger, he clutches with his whole body. It is no good
trying to take a particular anxiety and hand it over to
God, saying, 'Here, please take this bit of me and deal
with it, get rid of it for me.' We have got to take our
whole self and hand it over, the anxiety with all the rest,
and then he can carry it with us. It was only those who
were seeking first the kingdom of God that Jesus told not
to be anxious because their heavenly Father knew what
they needed and would give it to them.

Offering one's whole self is of course a very dangerous
thing to do. One of the many paradoxes of the Christian
faith is that we can only find relief from anxiety by
going into danger, for once we are committed to following
Christ we are committed to living as dangerously and
recklessly as he did. Jesus makes it clear again and again
that the one fatal thing to do is to try and cling on to
our notion of safety. I believe that this element of risk
in the Christian life meets a psychological need for danger
which does not get a proper outlet in the lives of many
people today. Children have a natural longing for the thrill
of danger. They look into dark cupboards or climb trees
or jump off something high. We are now beginning to
recognize this longing by providing outward-bound courses
and similar experiences for young people. But the need
for danger persists throughout our lives and too often as
we get older we try to meet it vicariously by watching
professional sportsmen risking their lives or by enjoying
a thriller on television.

But Christians cannot play for safety, and those who
are held by God can afford to be daring. Some are called
to go out and meet danger in obvious ways, encountering
the hatred and sickness and depression of people in desperate need. Others are called to face and deal with some
much less obvious danger. If you are very rich it could
be much more dangerous to live with the money and try

to use it properly and responsibly than to give it all away. Or if you are an assembly-line worker in a factory it could be much riskier going on there, trying to be Christ in that place and to bring his healing to a system that turns men into machines, than escaping into an easy, less destructive job.

Of course, if you are following Christ you will find danger in whatever your vocation turns out to be, just as you will also find the drudgery and pain, and the joy and fulfilment of carrying a cross. It is possible to serve him wherever you are and whatever your work happens to be. Social workers and clergy and teachers are not doing a more 'Christian' job than bus conductors or civil servants or bricklayers – in fact they may have a softer option. It can be most terrifyingly difficult to learn to find meaning in life and to see God and serve him when you are living and working in the greed and pressure and ugliness of industrial and commercial life. On the other hand, it does not follow that it is easy to be a Christian if you are living in beautiful surroundings. There is an old joke about a nature mystic who was rhapsodizing about the beauties of the earth to a ploughman and the ploughman's comment is, 'I looks at the bloody earth and I says bugger it.' Too close a contact with nature can be bloody in every sense of the word. I have worked as a shepherd and a farm labourer myself and I know.

But it is possible to learn to see God everywhere if one really starts looking for him; in the stable, solid squatness of a gasometer or the soaring of a concrete skyscraper or the tremendous engineering complexity of a vast spaghetti junction on a motorway or even the roar and power of a heavy motorbike. Perhaps also it is our particular vocation in the twentieth century to learn to find God in the starkness and noise and dirt of our industrial cities. Jesus emptied himself of beauty and the world is being emptied of natural beauty – we are being driven away from any escape into sentimentality, and our noses are being rubbed in what man produces when he makes production his god.

As I said at the beginning of this chapter, how any individual works out his vocation as a Christian is in the end his responsibility and his choice. The question always is, 'How do *I* follow Christ, here where I am?' 'How can the Lord the Spirit work in *this* place to make men and women more whole? How can love grow *here*, in this factory, this home, this office, this school?' And because we are unique, because there is no one who can take our particular place in creation, if you or I do not find the answer and act upon it, nobody will.

Also available in the Fontana Religious Series

What is Real in Christianity?
DAVID L. EDWARDS

The author strips away the legends from Jesus to show the man who is real, relevant and still fascinating. A clear, confident statement of Christian faith taking account of all criticisms.

The First Christmas
H. J. RICHARDS

Can one really believe in the seventies in such improbable events as the Virgin Birth, the shepherds and the angels, the Magi and the star in the East? Are they just fables? This book suggests that they might be the wrong questions to ask, and may even prevent the reader from arriving at the deeper issues. What these deeper issues are is here explained with clarity, simplicity and honesty.

Wrestling with Christ
LUIGI SANTUCCI

'This is a most unusual book, a prolonged meditation of the life of Christ using many changing literary forms, dialogue, description, addresses to Christ, passages of self-communing. It is written by a Christian passionately concerned that everyone should know Jesus Christ.'   *Catholic Herald*

Journey for a Soul
GEORGE APPLETON

'Wherever you turn in this inexpensive but extraordinarily valuable paperback you will benefit from sharing this man's pilgrimage of the soul.'

Methodist Recorder